Mental Health & Mental Capacity Law for Social Workers

SAGE was founded in 1965 by Sara Miller McCune to support
the dissemination of usable knowledge by publishing innovative
and high-quality research and teaching content. Today, we
publish more than 850 journals, including those of more than
300 learned societies, more than 800 new books per year, and
a growing range of library products including archives, data,
case studies, reports, and video. SAGE remains majority-owned
by our founder, and after Sara's lifetime will become owned by
a charitable trust that secures our continued independence.

Los Angeles | London | New Delhi | Singapore | Washington DC

Mental Health & Mental Capacity Law for Social Workers

An Introduction

Simon Godefroy

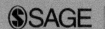

Los Angeles | London | New Delhi
Singapore | Washington DC

Series Editors:
Jonathan Parker and Greta Bradley

Learning Matters
An imprint of SAGE Publications Ltd
1 Oliver's Yard
55 City Road
London EC1Y 1SP

SAGE Publications Inc.
2455 Teller Road
Thousand Oaks, California 91320

SAGE Publications India Pvt Ltd
B 1/I 1 Mohan Cooperative Industrial Area
Mathura Road
New Delhi 110 044

SAGE Publications Asia-Pacific Pte Ltd
3 Church Street
#10-04 Samsung Hub
Singapore 049483

Editor: Kate Wharton
Production controller: Chris Marke
Project management: Swales & Willis Ltd,
Exeter, Devon
Marketing manager: Tamara Navaratnam
Cover design: Wendy Scott
Typeset by: C&M Digitals (P) Ltd, Chennai, India
Printed and bound in Great Britain by Ashford Colour
Press Ltd.

Library of Congress Control Number: 2015937417

British Library Cataloguing in Publication Data

A catalogue record for this book is available from the
British Library

ISBN 978-1-4462-8278-6
ISBN 978-1-4462-8279-3 (pbk)

At SAGE we take sustainability seriously. Most of our products are printed in the UK using FSC papers and boards.
When we print overseas we ensure sustainable papers are used as measured by the Egmont grading system.
We undertake an annual audit to monitor our sustainability.

In memory of

Hazel Irene Patterson

11 August 1941–2 November 2012

Contents

About the author

Simon Godefroy is the Programme Director of the London and Thames Valley Approved Mental Health Professional (AMHP) Programmes for Bournemouth University. Having started out as a probation officer and substance misuse social worker, Simon qualified as an approved social worker in 2000, and is currently practising as a locum social worker, AMHP and best interests assessor. Until August 2012 he was employed by Wokingham Borough Council as the AMHP and Forensic Lead. Simon is a Mental Health Act Reviewer for the Care Quality Commission. He is also an independent trainer and consultant specialising in various aspects of working with mentally disordered offenders and working with the Mental Capacity Act 2005 as well as providing AMHP and BIA supervision. He publishes a monthly digest on social work, mental health and related law on Twitter.

Acknowledgements

This book is dedicated to the memory of my mother who died from bowel cancer at the age of 71. If it were not for her efforts to ensure I received a proper education, this book would not have been written. I was born partially deaf, something my mother really began to notice when my sister came along a couple of years later and started to learn to speak. However, she could not get doctors to listen to her concerns, and it was not until the age of four that I was diagnosed and fitted with ugly body-worn hearing aids. My parents were warned that I would leave school with no qualifications, something that was not acceptable to my mother. I was sent to a special school for deaf children at the age of five but by the age of eight, whilst I was able to speak, I did not know what the alphabet was. I was summarily transferred into mainstream education and my mother made me read a book a week for several years to bring my reading skills to the level of my peers. When I reached my teenage years she arranged for me to see a speech therapist for several years to ensure that I could communicate clearly in readiness for the world of work. I eventually managed to obtain two degrees and I am in the final stages of my third. If it was not for the determination of my late mother, I would not be where I am today and for that I owe her my eternal gratitude.

I have been inspired as a social worker and as an approved social worker/approved mental health professional by having the privilege to work as part of some dedicated and passionate mental health and social care teams in my career. Professionals in mental health and in social care rarely get the sort of acknowledgement they deserve. I want to thank all the staff of the Wokingham Community Mental Health Team which I have been proud to be a part of for ten years. Also to the staff of the Berkshire Emergency Duty Service who strive to provide a high-quality, integrated social work and social care service out of hours: thank you.

I also want to thank several people who have helped with the book. Thanks to Luke Block and Kate Wharton, Commissioning Editors at Sage, for taking a punt on a new author. I want to thank Helen Fairlie, my editor, whose advice, support and encouragement has been invaluable. Thanks are also due to my colleagues at Bournemouth University and others for their helpful comments and advice on chapters of the book: Louize Collins, Mark Veldmeijer, Jo Parker, Karen Paige and Gareth Davies. Thanks to Professor Jonathan Parker for his useful comments on the text.

Finally, but by no means least, I would like to thank my long-suffering partner Tony Short for his support and encouragement with the project, oh, and for designing the diagrams in Chapter 1.

Simon Godefroy
March 2015

Introduction

This book aims to provide an introductory text for social workers, students on qualifying courses (as well as those on post-qualifying programmes) and other professionals on mental health and mental capacity law. Students, qualified social workers and other professionals can struggle with the complexities of mental health and mental capacity law (and law in general) and introductory textbooks are thin on the ground. There are books aimed at qualified and experienced mental health professionals as part of approved mental health professional and best interests assessor training but few for people starting out in this area of law.

This book will focus on the application of law to social work practice with adults. It aims to provide a good level of understanding of mental health and mental capacity law as required for social work practice at qualifying level. It is written to be readable and accessible. Do not make the mistake of thinking that this area of law is interesting for social workers to know about, but does not have any real application until you undertake further training. Whatever area of social work or health/social care you work in, you will encounter people in mental distress and/or those who may lack capacity to make decisions about their care. To be effective in caring for these people you will need a good working understanding of mental health and mental capacity law and the situations to which it may apply.

The focus of the book is about the practical application of the law in situations you will face as a social worker, so there are exercises and case studies to enable you to think about how you will apply the law in practice. The book starts with an introduction to law by asking the question, 'what is the law?' We will move on to consider the historical basis to mental health, mental capacity and human rights law and how it has developed to what we have now. Consideration will be given to the complexities of the definition of mental disorder including an exploration of a range of models of mental disorder. It will then explore in more depth core aspects of the law and practice issues with application of principles and values as a central thread.

This book is organised in three parts. Chapters 1 to 3 provide an introduction to mental health and the law. Chapters 4 to 7 focus on applying the law within social work practice. Chapters 8 to 10 examine provisions with regard to mentally disordered offenders, the Deprivation of Liberty Safeguards and safeguards for people who come within the provisions of the Mental Health Act 1983 and the Mental Capacity Act 2005.

Part I: Introduction to mental health and the law

Chapter 1: What is the law?
This chapter introduces the key legal concepts that we will be considering throughout the book and provides a foundation for your understanding of this area of law.

We explore how law is made and the different types of law from primary legislation and secondary legislation through to common law and case law. It briefly introduces the idea of 'the rule of law' as it applies to social workers and then goes on to introduce the European Convention on Human Rights (ECHR) and the Human Rights Act 1998.

Chapter 2: Historical perspectives
In order to understand the current issues in mental health law, it is important we briefly consider the historical context. This chapter also explores the development of a range of models of mental disorder as well as charting the development of the legal understanding of mental capacity though case law and statute. This includes the development of the law around 'valid consent'.

Chapter 3: Introduction to the Mental Health Act 1983 and the Mental Capacity Act 2005
This chapter provides an overview of the Mental Health Act 1983 (MHA) and the Mental Capacity Act 2005 (MCA) as well as later amendments. It examines in detail section 1 of the Mental Health Act and the definition of mental disorder as well as the aims and function of this Act. It also introduces the definition of mental incapacity in section 2 of the Mental Capacity Act and how this is assessed in section 3. This will enable you to understand the gateways into these two pieces of legislation so that you will understand how people come within their provisions. We introduce the role of the three statutory Codes of Practice which apply to these Acts. This chapter concludes with an outline of the key roles within these two pieces of legislation and commonly used abbreviations.

Part II: Application to practice

Chapter 4: Principles and values
The principles that underpin the application of these two Acts will be introduced, linking them both to the ECHR and social work professional standards. We introduce some key ethical dilemmas that arise within mental health law including the key tension between 'care and control'. Connections are made in this chapter between the application of mental health law and the social work value base. Promoting the rights and full participation of people who have a mental disorder and/or lack capacity to make decisions regarding their care is essential within this area of law but raises some very key challenges.

Chapter 5: Assessment
How people are assessed under these two Acts and the processes involved (except under the Deprivation of Liberty Safeguards, which is left to Chapter 9) forms the focus of this chapter. The process of the Mental Health Act assessment and the key roles are explored with a focus on sections 2, 3, 4, 135, 136, 6 and 13. We also revisit how mental capacity to make a specific decision is assessed under the Mental Capacity Act.

Chapter 6: Providing care
Here we focus on the provision of care as authorised under the Mental Health Act and Mental Capacity Act. The provision of 'medical treatment' under the MHA is explored with a focus on the Mental Health Act guiding principles. What treatment

can be provided under the MHA and what cannot be provided under this Act is examined. The role of independent mental health advocate (IMHA) is explored.

We then go on to explore best interest decision making under the MCA and examine the protection for those making decisions under the MCA. We consider the legal basis for the use of restraint under the MCA. Advance decisions are also discussed. The chapter ends by introducing the role of the independent mental capacity advocate (IMCA).

Chapter 7: Care outside of hospital

The focus is now on moving care away from the hospital setting to the community with an examination of guardianship, section 17 leave and community treatment orders and the provision of aftercare. We continue to be focused on the application of principles and social work values to ensure that you are able to understand the key tensions between promoting independence and autonomy whilst keeping people safe.

Part III: Other provisions and safeguards

Chapter 8: Mentally disordered offenders

People who are in mental distress at times come into contact with the criminal justice system. This chapter explores the concept of diversion and the role of mental health and medical professionals in dealing with people in police custody. It outlines the key provisions of Part III MHA with regard to mentally disordered offenders. This chapter aims to better inform professionals who support people within the criminal justice system.

Chapter 9: Deprivation of Liberty Safeguards (DOLS)

This chapter introduces the DOLS, what is a deprivation of liberty, the key roles within DOLS and the six qualifying assessments. This chapter aims to provide a basic introduction to this complicated and sometimes difficult to understand area of law. The purpose of this is to raise awareness of what might constitute a deprivation of liberty so that you can take the appropriate action.

Chapter 10: Safeguards

There are key safeguards for people who come within the provisions of the MHA and the MCA. This chapter explains what rights people have and how they can exercise those rights. These include the role of the nearest relative, the hospital managers, the Mental Health Tribunal and the Care Quality Commission for those under the MHA. It also considers the Lasting Power of Attorney, the role of Court of Protection appointed deputies, the relevant person's representative, and the Court of Protection for those under the MCA.

This book has incorporated the recently implemented (April 2015) Mental Health Act Code of Practice and its Reference Guide. At the same time a major legislative change in the provision of social care services in the form of the Care Act 2014 was implemented. This Act has combined a range of social care provisions going back to the National Assistance Act 1948 into one overarching Act of Parliament for the first time. Its impact on the provision of social services is profound. However, this book does not explore this

Act in any detail except where there are specific changes to the Mental Health Act and how its provisions fit within existing mental health and mental capacity law.

This book has been carefully mapped to the Professional Capabilities Framework for Social Workers in England and will help you to develop the appropriate standards at the right level. These standards are:

- **Professionalism**
  Identify and behave as a professional social worker committed to professional development.

- **Values and ethics**
  Apply social work ethical principles and values to guide professional practice.

- **Diversity**
  Recognise diversity and apply anti-discriminatory and anti-oppressive principles in practice.

- **Rights, justice and economic well-being**
  Advance human rights and promote social justice and economic well-being.

- **Knowledge**
  Apply knowledge of social sciences, law and social work practice theory.

- **Critical reflection and analysis**
  Apply critical reflection and analysis to inform and provide a rationale for professional decision-making.

- **Intervention and skills**
  Use judgement and authority to intervene with individuals, families and communities to promote independence, provide support and prevent harm, neglect and abuse.

- **Contexts and organisations**
  Engage with, inform, and adapt to changing contexts that shape practice. Operate effectively within your own organisational frameworks and contribute to the development of services and organisations. Operate effectively within multi-agency and inter-professional settings.

- **Professional leadership**
  Take responsibility for the professional learning and development of others through supervision, mentoring, assessing, research, teaching, leadership and management.

References to these standards will be made throughout the text and you will find a diagram of the Professional Capabilities Framework in an appendix on page 161.

Part I
Introduction to mental health and the law

Chapter 1
What is the law?

A C H I E V I N G   A   S O C I A L   W O R K   D E G R E E

This chapter will help you to develop the following capabilities from the Professional Capabilities Framework:

- **Professionalism**
  Identify and behave as a professional social worker committed to professional development.

- **Values and ethics**
  Apply social work ethical principles and values to guide professional practice.

- **Rights, justice and economic well-being**
  Advance human rights and promote social justice and economic well-being.

- **Knowledge**
  Apply the knowledge of social sciences, law and social work practice theory.

- **Intervention and skills**
  Use judgement and authority to intervene with individuals, families and communities to promote independence, provide support and prevent harm, neglect and abuse.

It will also help you develop the following National Occupational Standards for Social Work in Wales:

- **Maintain professional accountability**
  SW 1: Maintain an up-to-date knowledge and evidence base for social work practice.

- **Practise professional social work**
  SW 4: Exercise professional judgement in social work.

- **Promote engagement and participation**
  SW 9: Engage people in social work practice.
  SW 10: Support people to participate in decision-making processes.
  SW 11: Advocate on behalf of people.

Introduction

The study and understanding of the law can create anxieties for even the most experienced social worker. For student social workers it can be difficult to know where to start. Most law books start from the expectation that their readers will have a basic grounding in law, and as a result they are not always easy for social workers to read and understand. Law books that are written from a social work perspective are usually aimed at experienced social workers who are undertaking specialist training in this area, and as a result they are not always easily accessible for student and newly qualified social workers. This book starts from the premise that you do not know anything about the law. It seeks to give you a grounding in the law and to guide you through to the point where you feel you have a basic understanding of how law works.

Many social workers try to avoid reading or studying the law. This is a grave mistake. The social worker's fundamental duties and powers are set out in law. This includes the Care Act 2014, which seeks to bring social care law up to date by combining powers and duties spread across several Acts of Parliament into one overarching piece of legislation. You need to keep abreast of legal developments as they relate to working with vulnerable adults, and adults with mental health problems, in order to ensure that you continue to practise lawfully.

Before we go on to examine the Mental Health Act 1983 and Mental Capacity Act 2005 in detail, we need to ensure that we understand the fundamentals of law. What is the law? Who makes the law? How do we read and understand the law? Once we understand the basics, we can go on to examine how the law applies to social workers, and how you should use and apply the law.

This chapter aims to equip you with the basic skills to read, understand and apply the law to your work. We will start by looking at the two main sources of law: legislation and case law. We will then explore how you can find, read and understand different types of law. Following this we will briefly explore how the court system works before examining the differing ways that law is applied and enforced. Finally we will look at the Human Rights Act and how you need to have regard to it in the application of the law.

What is the law?

A simple and easy to understand definition of law is:

> The system of rules which a particular country or community recognizes as regulating the actions of its members and which it may enforce by the imposition of penalties.

> (Oxford Dictionaries, 2014)

If the law is to be understood as a system of rules, which regulates the actions of citizens of a country, then living under the law is called 'the rule of law'. Tom Bingham, a former British senior law lord, has written a very accessible book explaining what the rule of law means. It is not a long book, and it should be in the library of every social worker who believes in the importance of human rights and the rule of law. In his book, Bingham (2010: p8) defines the rule of law as:

> The core of the existing principle is, I suggest, that all persons and authorities within the state, whether public or private, should be bound by and entitled to the benefit of laws publicly made, taking effect (generally) in the future and publicly administered in the courts.

We can see that everyone is subject to the rule of law and when social workers carry out their statutory duties they must do so lawfully or they, and the public authorities on whose behalf they work, will fall foul of the law.

In the United Kingdom we have several separate legal jurisdictions. Scotland has its own legal system with its own laws and court system. So does Northern Ireland. Throughout this book we will focus on the laws and legal systems as they apply in England and Wales as the Mental Health Act 1983 and the Mental Capacity Act 2005 only apply in these two countries of the United Kingdom.

The law as it applies in England and Wales cannot only be found written down in a legal text. The law is found in the following sources:

- **Legislation passed by the Houses of Parliament.** These are known as statutes or Acts of Parliament. This is where we get the term 'statutory', meaning set out in statute.

- **Common law.** This is law that is not the result of legislation. It is law developed by cases as decided by judges in the courts of England and Wales.

- **Case law.** This is law that is developed as judges and courts seek to interpret what Parliament intended in passing statutes. Case law helps us to understand how the law should be applied.

There are other sources of law such as those made by the European Union and International Conventions, but these are outside the scope of this book. However, later in the chapter, we will examine one important piece of European law which has a powerful effect on the work of social workers practising in the UK: the European Convention on Human Rights.

Because the legal system in England and Wales is made up of both legislation and case law, it is called a common law system. It is important, therefore, that social workers are able to understand both legislation and case law in order to successfully understand and comply with the law in their work. We need to now explore these different sources of law in more detail.

Legislation

Primary legislation

Primary legislation is that which is passed by Parliament in the form of statutes or Acts of Parliament. The name of a statute always ends with the word 'Act' and the year in which it was passed. The Mental Health Act 1983 and Mental Capacity Act 2005 are examples of statutes or primary legislation. It is important to include the date when citing statutes because there are Acts of Parliament with the same name but passed in different years, for example the Mental Health Act 1983 and the Mental Health Act 2007 as well as the Children Act 1989 and the Children Act 2004.

Legislation starts its life in the form of a bill that is introduced in one of the Houses of Parliament: the House of Lords or the House of Commons. Finch and Fafinski (2009: pp13–15) set out the process through which a bill becomes law. Most bills start their life in the House of Commons and go through the first and second readings in the House before moving on to the committee stage, which examines the provisions of the bill in detail. The bill as amended at this stage goes back to the Commons for its third reading. Once it passes the third reading it then moves on to the House of Lords. The procedure in the Lords is basically the same as the Commons with the bill returning to the Commons for any amendments introduced by the Lords to be considered by the Commons. If the House of Commons does not agree with the amendments it can send it back to the Lords for reconsideration. As a result a bill can find itself being passed back and forth several times before being agreed by both Houses of Parliament. Once a bill is passed by both Houses it needs to receive Royal Assent before it becomes law. An Act can come into force on the day it receives Royal Assent or it can come into force on a later day. For example the Mental Health Act 2007 received Royal Assent on 19 July 2007 but most of its provisions did not come into force until 3 November 2008 (Mental Health Law Online, 2013).

Secondary legislation

Secondary legislation is also known as delegated legislation and is defined as 'law made by persons or bodies with the delegated authority of Parliament' (Finch and Fafinski, 2009: p15). Secondary legislation is the law as enacted usually by Government ministers. Ministers cannot enact law for which they have not been given the power by Parliament, and only then in specific circumstances allowed for in the enabling Act of Parliament. The advantage of secondary legislation is that it can contain detail that is considered too complex to include in an Act of Parliament. It can also be changed more easily without going through the process of introducing a new bill through Parliament. On the other hand, secondary legislation can be changed without a full debate in Parliament.

Examples of secondary legislation include the Mental Health (Approved Mental Health Professionals) (Approval) (England) Regulations 2008, which sets out the professional requirements and competencies that approved mental health professionals need to achieve before they can be approved.

Common law and case law

As we have already stated, common law is law that is based on the decisions of courts over time. It is usually taken to mean the law that is not the result of legislation; it is the law that derives from cases decided by judges and the value of the judicial precedents that these decisions set (Finch and Fafinski, 2009: p99). We can see, therefore, that common law fills in the gaps left by Parliament. Some examples of common law doctrines that are well established in our law but are not in statute include: the offence of murder (you will find the punishment for murder in statute but not the actual offence itself), the doctrine of confidentiality and the doctrine of duty of care.

There are situations where Parliament decides that common law doctrine needs to be incorporated into statute. The Mental Capacity Act 2005 definition of mental capacity is a good example of this and we will explore this in more detail in the next chapter.

Case law involves judges interpreting the intention of Parliament in passing a particular statute. It is important for social workers to understand that case law is the application of the law by judges to a given set of facts, in a particular case that is before the court. Two cases, which on the face of it appear to be very similar, can lead to two very different decisions by the judges involved. In two separate cases involving two women with severe eating disorders, *E* (*A Local Authority v E and Ors* [2012] EWHC 1639 (COP)) and *L* (*The NHS Trust v L and Ors* [2012] EWHC 2741 (COP)), there were two very different outcomes even though the facts of each case were similar. Both women needed forced Artificial Nutrition and Hydration (ANH) if they were to stay alive. Both were found to lack the mental capacity to make this decision, so the courts had to decide if this medical treatment was in their best interests. In the case of *E* the judge ruled that she should have forced ANH but in the case of *L* the judge ruled that she should not and be allowed to die. It appears on reading these two cases that the only substantial difference between them is the futility or otherwise of the treatment, i.e. that in one case the proposed treatment had a chance of success but in the other case the treatment was very likely to be unsuccessful.

How to find and read legislation

Where to find statute

There are several ways that you can find and read statutes. Often you will find Acts of Parliament reproduced in guides or manuals covering that particular Act or area of law (e.g. Barber et al., 2012 or Jones, 2013, both covering mental health law). These can be a good source of law for social workers; as well as including the text of the Act (with all the amendments included), they offer guidance to readers to enable you to better understand the law in this area.

Students and qualified social workers may be able to access law databases through their local academic library. Databases such as Lawtel, Lexis Library and Westlaw provide full access to full texts of all the Acts of Parliament that are currently in force (including the amendments). These databases provide a range of features so that the provisions of these statues can be explored in more detail, linking to relevant cases, journal articles and books.

There is also a range of publicly accessible websites in which you can access statutes. The Government has its own public access database of legislation (**www.legislation. gov.uk**), which is free to use. However, sometimes the legislation is not up to date but there are warnings if there are outstanding changes that need to be made. You can download a PDF of the Act, but it is generally the Act as originally enacted and does not include amendments made by subsequent legislation.

Another very useful website is Mental Health Law Online (**www.mentalheathlaw.co.uk**). This site is a resource for mental health practitioners and includes access to the full text of relevant statutes and Codes of Practice as well as relevant case law. The text of the Mental Health Act 1983 is broken down by section with links to case law, the

Mental Health Act Code of Practice (Department of Health, 2015a) and the Reference Guide to the Mental Health Act (Department of Health, 2015b). It is very useful source of information on mental health and mental capacity law.

Looking up a statute

Search for the Mental Capacity Act 2005 on some of the databases mentioned above. Note how different databases give you extra information about the Act, such as when it came into force and details of amendments. Which ones appear to be more useful to you?

How to read statute

In order to learn how to read statute you need to understand how an Act is organised and structured. There may some variation between different Acts but the general structure is usually as follows.

The front page contains the title, the date the Act received Royal Assent and the arrangement of the sections of the Act. This is the contents page of the Act and gives a useful overview of what the Act contains.

Below the title you will see a date followed by the chapter number. In the case of the Mental Health Act 1983 you will see '1983 Chapter 20'. This means that this was the 20th Act to be given Royal Assent in 1983.

Then follows a longer title of the Act, which explains the purpose of the Act.

You will then find the body of the Act itself. It may be divided into Parts with a title explaining what that Part covers. By convention Parts are numbered using roman numerals. The Part number is not used when citing legislation unless you are referring to the Part as a whole, e.g. Part III of the Mental Health Act 1983 covering the provisions for mentally disordered offenders.

The main building blocks of an Act of Parliament are sections and these are usually cited by using an abbreviation (s1, s2, etc.). Sections are further divided by sub-sections using numbers in parentheses (s1(1), s1(2), etc.). If required, sub-sections can be further divided into paragraphs, using lower case letters again within parentheses (s1(1)(a), s1(1)(b), etc.). Very occasionally you will find paragraphs divided into sub-paragraphs and these are designated by lower case roman numerals again within parentheses (s1(1)(a)(iii), s2(b)(c)(iv), etc.). You will sometimes come across a section or sub-section number followed by a capital letter e.g. s17A or s1(2A). These are sections and sub-sections inserted by amending legislation. The Mental Health Act 2007 added the above sections and sub-sections to the Mental Health Act 1983. You will also see brackets showing where legalisation has been amended. For example [. . .]

shows where sections have been removed by later legislation and [approved mental health professional] shows a phrase that has been added.

At the end of the Act you may find schedules designated by number and divided into paragraphs and sub-paragraphs.

Secondary legislation is usually in the form of a statutory instrument and is usually organised in a similar way to an Act of Parliament but the main building blocks are rules or regulations rather than sections (cited r1, r2, etc.). Just to be confusing rules are divided into sub-sections not sub-rules!

When reading legislation there are some features that will seem anachronistic and out of date especially for social workers. A person is always referred to in the male gender so you will find references to 'him' and 'himself' but not 'her' or 'herself'. It is legal convention that references to the male gender refer to both genders. When quoting legislation social workers need to stick to this legal convention, no matter how much it goes against the grain. Baroness Hale addresses this issue in the preface to her excellent book on mental health law:

> Most mental health professionals are women, so I have made them female in the text. Most mental health patients are men, so I have made them male. It helps distinguish the two. But no disrespect to either sex is intended.

> (Hale, 2010: p vii)

When reading her book as a male mental health professional it is an interesting experience being referred to in the female gender. It makes you wonder when Parliament will catch up with the rest of society and find a more inclusive way of writing legislation. Maybe that was Baroness Hale's intention in using this convention in her book.

However, references to gender are not the only anachronisms in reading the law. The Mental Health Act 1983 refers to 'patients', which is considered a medical label, and is a term that is subject to critique (Tew, 2005). Again when referring to people who come within the provisions of the Mental Health Act, this book will use the term 'patient' because that is the legal term used. The Mental Health Act also refers to 'mental disorder' so this term will also be used throughout this book. We will explore the meaning of 'mental disorder' in Chapter 3 and examine a range of models of mental disorder in Chapter 2.

ACTIVITY 1.2

Reading a statute

Find the Mental Health Act 1983 either in a handbook or via online databases. Note the structure of the Act as set out above. Look up section 3 of the Act and identify the section, sub-sections and paragraphs.

How to find and read case law

Whilst legislation should be drafted in simple and easy to read terms, it can be seen that this often is not the case as the legislation attempts to cover all possible eventualities. In reading case law you will see how courts and judges have attempted to interpret the law and apply it to the facts of the case before them. Therefore, the ability to find and read case law is an important skill for a social worker.

How to find a law report

In order for cases to be understood and decisions followed, cases in certain courts are reported. This relates to cases decided in the High Court, Court of Appeal or House of Lords (now replaced by the UK Supreme Court). There is a range of sources for reported cases and a full examination of these are beyond the scope of this book. Cases are reported in law reports and more latterly there are easily available official transcripts of cases produced by the courts.

In order to find a case in the law report, it is necessary to know how to understand what is a case citation. In our adversarial system of law, a case usually requires at least two parties on opposite sides, e.g. party A versus party B. The word 'versus' is abbreviated to 'v' in case citations, but when spoken about the 'v' or 'versus' is not said but replaced by an 'and' to designate the two parties in a case. There may be more than two parties in a case but these will usually be placed in two groups opposing each other. The person bringing the case (often known as the claimant or applicant) is cited first, followed by the person against whom the case is being brought (often known as the defendant or respondent). In many cases relating to a vulnerable adult, the name of the vulnerable adult (and other names which could lead to them being identified) are confidential. Usually, in such cases, a letter or letters replaces the names. The names of the parties are followed by a date and the details of the law report within which the case is found. An individual case is usually published in several law reports and then there is the official transcript, which will have its own citation. This is called the 'neutral citation' and most reported cases since 2001 will have a neutral citation. In order to reduce confusion this book will use the neutral citation when available and refer to the official transcript. However, it is often useful to read a case in a law report as well as the official transcript.

The neutral citation includes a unique number given to each judgment issued by the courts, which is a date followed by a series of letters and then a number. The series of letters refers to the court and then the division of the court that heard the case. These abbreviations are as follows:

EWHC – England and Wales High Court

EWCOP – England and Wales Court of Protection

EWCA – England and Wales Court of Appeal

UKHL – United Kingdom House of Lords

UKSC – United Kingdom Supreme Court

NEUTRAL CITATION
***Johnson v Short* [2009] EWHC 309 (Civ)**

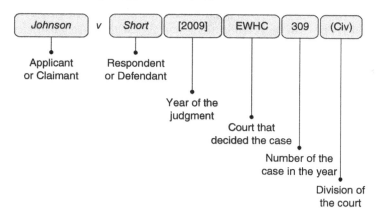

LAW REPORT CITATION
***Johnson v Short* [2009] 1 All ER 985**

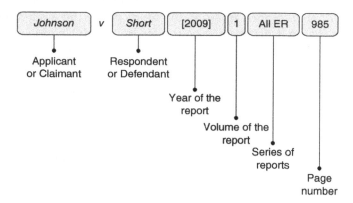

Figure 1.1 Law report citations explained

The High Court and Appeal Court divisions have abbreviations. The structure of the court system in England and Wales is discussed later in the chapter. These include:

Civ – Civil Division

Crim – Criminal Division

Admin – Administrative Court

COP – Court of Protection

There are a number of other divisions of the High Court but these are the ones that social workers are more likely to come across.

If we now look at a very important case in the area of mental capacity law and the Deprivation of Liberty Safeguards, the neutral citation is:

LB Hillingdon v Steven Neary [2011] EWHC 1377 (COP)

By reading this we see, by referring to Figure 1.1, that the applicant is the London Borough of Hillingdon, the respondent is Steven Neary (this case is unusual in that the name of the vulnerable adult has been made public), the case was decided in 2011, and was the 1377th case reported in that year. Whilst the case was heard in the High Court, the '(COP)' indicates that it was heard in the Court of Protection. In some cases the 'EWHC' and '(COP)' is replaced by 'EWCOP' but both show that it was a Court of Protection case.

It is also reported in several law reports, one of the more important of these being the All England Law Reports. It is cited there as:

Hillingdon London Borough Council v Neary [2011] 4 All ER 584

The number following the date indicates that it is the fourth volume of the law report in that year and the report starts on page 584 of that volume.

We can see from these citations that the London Borough of Hillingdon was the applicant (i.e. brought the case to the court) and Steven Neary was the respondent. In this case the reality was that Steven Neary was unhappy about the actions of Hillingdon but Hillingdon brought the case so that the courts could decide the matter. The courts prefer the local authority to bring a case to the courts where there is a dispute with a service user rather than put that burden on the service user. Hillingdon were criticised by the court for the delay in bringing the case (*LB Hillingdon v Steven Neary* [2011] EWHC 1377 (COP) para 32).

Once the system of case citations are understood, you can find the cases you are looking for. Law reports can be found in printed form in academic libraries, especially in those universities with a law school. However, many law reports are now available online, via subscription based databases such as Lawtel, Lexis Library and Westlaw, as discussed above. These databases include additional information on the cases reported, including links to the law reports, related cases and journal articles that can help you understand the importance of the case and how to apply it to your work or see if the decision has been overturned by a higher court. These databases also link to the official transcript where available. However, there are publicly available websites through which you can access case law. The most comprehensive of these is the British and Irish Legal Information Institute (**www.bailii.org**) and includes court decisions in the countries that make up the UK as well as European Union case law and Law Commission reports. It is dependent on donations to fund the costs of developing and maintaining its website. You will also find case law on Mental Health Law Online with links to transcripts on BAILII as well as other resources and information.

ACTIVITY **1.3**

Looking up a law report

Look up the Neary case cited above on one of the databases we have mentioned. Search for the case using the names of the parties. Conduct another search based on either the neutral citation or the law report citation.

How to read a law report

Like legislation, law reports are not always easy to read and the judge's reasoning behind their decisions is often difficult to follow. Reading case law, as with legislation, is a skill that takes time and practice to learn. The advantage of using databases and the websites cited above is that there are links to articles and other resources which can help you to understand what the judge is saying and why.

As with legislation, most law reports have a similar structure and when this is understood, it makes it a little easier to understand what is being said in the report. Law reports usually include:

- the court that is hearing the case

- the case name

- the case citation

- date of the hearing and the judgment

- the judge(s) hearing the case

- the judgment

The judgment is often the most difficult to read and, as Finch and Fafinski (2009: p150) explain, it usually (but not always) can be broken down into four sections: summary of the material facts of the case, statement of the applicable law, legal reasoning and the decision. It is useful when reading a case report to break down what is being read into one of these four sections.

The starting point in any case is the facts. The parties may or may not dispute the facts. The dispute between the parties may be on a point of law or what is the correct course of action. If the facts are not in dispute then the judge will merely set out the facts before setting out the relevant law as it applies to these facts. If the facts are disputed, then the judge will need to come to a decision on what they understand the facts to be and why, before going on to set out the relevant law. Once the judges have set out the facts and the law, they will then apply the law to the issue on which the court is being asked to decide. It is important that the reader understands the reason behind the case coming to court and what decision the court is being asked to make. Once the court has applied its legal reasoning it will set out its decision and the reasons for it.

A case will usually contain a central principle of law, which has been applied to the particular facts in the case in order for the judge to arrive at the decision that they did. It is useful, if possible, when reading a case report to determine what this principle was. The application of this principle central to the decision is called the 'ratio' and it is defined by Finch and Fafinski (2009: p157) as 'the legal rule and associated reasoning that is essential to the resolution of the case. It is the conclusion that is reached by the application of the relevant legal rule to the material facts'. If it is possible to draw out from the reading of the case the ratio on which the case is resolved, then you will be in a much better position to apply this legal principle or rule to other sets of facts and allow case law to inform your social work practice.

ACTIVITY 1.4

Reading a law report

Find the official transcript of the Neary case by using the neutral citation. Make sure you have found the later case (heard in June 2011) as there were two hearings. Read through the report and identify the following parts of the report:

- *the name of the court that heard the case*

- *the names of the applicant and the respondents*

- *the name of the judge hearing the case and giving the judgment*

- *the facts of the case*

- *what law applies to this case*

- *the judge's decision*

Once you have read through the law report, think about how the judgment may apply to your role as a social worker making decisions about the care of a person with a learning disability.

COMMENT

The key legal principle in this case was set out in paragraphs 22 and 23, which are about the limits of the ordinary powers of a local authority. Judge Jackson states that the ordinary powers of a local authority are limited to investigating, providing support and referring the matter to a court when appropriate. If you as a local authority social worker need to do more than this (that is, regulate, control, compel, restrain, etc.) then you need to point to a specific statutory authority for your actions or go to court.

How is the law applied, used and enforced?

The court system

In order to understand how the law works, it is important to have a working knowledge of the court system in England and Wales. Courts are divided into two types: criminal courts and civil courts. However, as Finch and Fafinski explain (2009: pp103–4) courts can also be divided between trial and appellate courts, as well as superior and inferior courts.

Criminal courts deal with people who are alleged to have committed criminal offences as set out in criminal law. These courts determine if those accused of offences (called defendants) are guilty or not guilty. If defendants are found guilty (convicted) then the courts punish these offenders according to the sanctions available to them. Criminal courts do have to deal with defendants and offenders who have mental disorders and they have certain powers to deal with them appropriately while protecting the public. These powers will be explored in Chapter 8.

Civil courts primarily deal with disputes between individuals and can apply remedies. These can be in the form of monetary damages but could also include declarations as to what actions should be taken or avoided. If there were a dispute between a local authority and a person over the provision of care, this would be settled by a civil court.

A trial court is the first court to hear a case (also called hearing at first instance) and make a decision, while an appellate court hears appeals from trial courts, usually where there is a dispute about a principle of law rather than fact.

Inferior courts refer to the lower courts that usually hear the more straightforward cases. Superior courts are the higher courts that hear the more difficult or important cases.

In England there is also a system of tribunals, which is now also administered by Her Majesty's Court and Tribunal Service. One of these tribunals is the Mental Health Tribunal, which hears applications from patients detained under the Mental Health Act 1983. This will be discussed in more detail in Chapter 10. The tribunal service is made up of the First Tier Tribunal and the Upper Tribunal. The First Tier Tribunal is equivalent to the trial court and the Upper Tribunal is equivalent to the appellate court. It is important

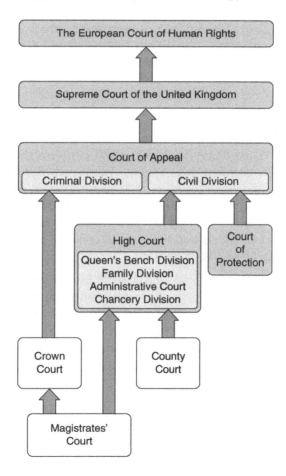

Figure 1.2 The hierarchy of the courts system in England and Wales

Adapted from Finch and Fafinski (2009: p103).

to note that the Upper Tribunal has the same status as the High Court and therefore its judgments can be published and have to be followed. Upper Tribunal case reports can be recognised by the neutral citation including the abbreviation UKUT.

The tribunal system is slightly different in Wales in that the Mental Health Review Tribunal still exists but appeals are still to the Upper Tribunal.

The reason why it is important to understand how the courts are structured is because of the principle of judicial precedent. This is based on the idea that the law needs to be applied consistently, i.e. cases with similar material facts should be treated the same. The way this is done is that the decisions of the higher courts in the hierarchy (as shown in Figure 1.2 above) have greater legal weight than the decisions of the lower courts when cases are concerned with the same legal issues. Higher court decisions are binding on the courts at the same level and below. However, decisions of the inferior courts (below the level of the High Court) are not binding. Therefore, a decision of the UK Supreme Court is binding on all UK courts whilst a decision of the High Court is only binding on the High Court and the courts below it: it is not binding on the Court of Appeal or the UK Supreme Court.

Therefore, when reading a law report it is important to know which court made the decision in order to understand the weight that needs to be given to that decision. The higher the court the more important is the legal rule (the ratio) as it has been applied to the facts of the case.

Judicial review

The law gives public officials the power to make certain decisions without having to go to court. This is called administrative law and concerns the decision making of public bodies and Government departments. These sort of decisions include those that social workers make in the course of their everyday work, such as assessments of need and provision of services. People who are affected by these decisions have the right to ask a court to review the way that the decision is made. This is called judicial review. It is important to understand that judicial review is a review of the process by which the public body arrived at its decision.

We can see that a decision of a social worker could be judicially reviewed. The doctrine of vicarious liability means that a social worker's employer would normally be liable in law for any shortcomings in the actions of its employee. Normally it would be the employer who would appear before the court but it is not unknown for individual social workers to find themselves subject to judicial review.

Finch and Fafinski (2009: p107) state that judicial review proceedings need to be based on one of the following three grounds:

1. Was the decision illegal? Has the public body failed to recognise and give effect to the law or have they acted outside their legal powers?

2. Was the decision irrational? Was the public body's decision so outrageous in its defiance of logic or accepted moral standards that no reasonable decision maker could have arrived at it?

3. Was the decision made following the proper procedures? This covers statutory procedural requirements as well as the common law rules of natural justice, e.g. were the decision makers biased, or did they fail to give a fair hearing?

If the court finds that the decision made by the public body was not lawful, it can quash the decision and ask the public body to go through the decision-making process again.

While judicial review is not the only way that social workers' decisions could end up being scrutinised by a court, you do need to understand the importance of making legal, rational decisions by following the proper procedures.

Duties and powers

The law gives social workers, usually by being employed by a local authority or other public body, certain powers and duties and these are discussed in detail throughout this book. These can stem from statute or from case law (the latter usually called common law powers or duties). However, it is important to be clear what the difference is between a power and a duty.

A power is something that is permitted, or something that may be done. Examples of statutory powers include the provision of residential accommodation under the Care Act 2014, making a decision regarding a care package for a person who lacks capacity to make that decision under the Mental Capacity Act 2005 (MCA), or making an application to detain a patient under the Mental Health Act 1983 (MHA). Common law powers include the power to restrain a person who lacks capacity to prevent them harming other people, if the provisions of the Mental Capacity Act cannot be used.

A duty is something that has to be done. Example of statutory duties include providing an assessment of a person's needs under the Care Act 2014 and taking the case of someone who appears to be mentally disordered under consideration if required to do so by their nearest relative under the Mental Health Act 1983. Common law duties include the duty of confidentiality and the duty of care.

ACTIVITY **1.5**

Powers and duties

You have been asked to assess a vulnerable adult following adult safeguarding referral. It has been reported to the local authority that an older woman who lives alone is being financially exploited by neighbours who come in to do tasks such as shopping and cleaning. Her son and her daughter provide all other care. In carrying out your assessment and considering what services this woman needs, what are your duties (what you must do) and what are your powers (things you are permitted to do)?

The impact of the Human Rights Act 1998

The Human Rights Act 1998 (HRA) came into force in October 2000 and had the effect of incorporating most of the European Convention on Human Rights (ECHR) into UK law. Jones (2013: 5–002) states that the Second World War and its associated horror caused an upsurge in international concern for human rights. The ECHR arose out of that concern. The Convention comes under the auspices of the Council of Europe and is completely separate from the European Union.

These were not new rights for people living in the UK, as it ratified the Convention in 1951 and it came into force in 1953. However, the Human Rights Act 1998 does make these rights more accessible. Public bodies (including social workers) have to act in accordance with the Convention rights (HRA 1998, s6), courts must interpret legislation in accordance with these rights (HRA 1998, s2), and individuals can now bring actions before UK courts complaining that their Convention rights have been breached (HRA 1998, s7). These rights are set out in the Convention as Articles and these are reproduced in Figure 1.3 below. Several of these rights will be discussed in more detail throughout the book.

	Article 2	Right to life
	Article 3	Prohibition of torture
	Article 4	Prohibition of slavery and forced labour
	Article 5	Right to liberty and security
	Article 6	Right to a fair trial
	Article 7	No punishment without law
	Article 8	Right to respect for private and family life
	Article 9	Freedom of thought, conscience and religion
	Article 10	Freedom of expression
	Article 11	Freedom of assembly and association
	Article 12	Right to marry
	Article 14	Prohibition of discrimination
Protocol 1	**Article 1**	Protection of property
Protocol 1	**Article 2**	Right to education
Protocol 1	**Article 3**	Right to free elections

Figure 1.3 Rights incorporated into UK law from the European Convention on Human Rights

The full text of these rights can been found by looking up the Human Rights Act on **www.legislation.gov.uk**, and The Equality and Human Rights Commission provide an easy to read guide to these Convention rights (**www.equalityhumanrights.com/ your-rights/human-rights/what-are-human-rights/human-rights-act**).

A full study of the implications of the Human Rights Act for social workers is beyond the scope of this book and it is expected that social workers should make themselves aware of its implications for their work. However, as we explore the provisions of the Mental Health Act and Mental Capacity Act in more detail we will be examining the impact of these Convention rights when applying these Acts.

CHAPTER SUMMARY

- The law is a system of rules that regulates the actions of citizens.

- The law in the United Kingdom is made up of legislation and case law.

- Legislation is the law as enacted by Parliament or Government ministers.

- Case law derives from cases as decided by judges over time as well as judges interpreting and applying legislation.

- Judicial review is the power of judges to review decisions by public bodies including social workers.

- The Human Rights Act 1998 incorporates most of the European Convention on Human Rights into UK law and social workers (as well as other public authorities) have to act in accordance with these Convention rights.

FURTHER READING

Bingham, T (2010) *The Rule of Law*. London: Penguin Books.

This is a very readable and accessible book that explains the importance of the rule of law.

Finch, E and Fafinski, S (2009) *Legal Skills*, 2nd edition. Oxford: Oxford University Press.

This book is aimed at law students. Part 1 of the book gives much more detail on sources of law.

Chapter 2
Historical perspectives

Introduction

In order to understand our present state of affairs it is often useful to know how we got here. In this chapter we will be looking at the development of the law around dealing with people with what we now call mental health problems and people with learning disabilities. This will serve to put our exploration of the current law into a historical context. It is interesting to understand what has changed over time, but more importantly, what has broadly remained the same. In exploring the development of mental health law we also see the rise of what was to become the social work profession, from the poor law relieving officers to the approved mental health professionals of the present day. We will begin to understand why social workers are involved in working with the mentally distressed and those who are not able to make decisions for themselves.

This chapter will explore the development of mental health law and show the rise of the involvement of non-medical professionals in this area of law. We will then explore the much more recent development of law around mental incapacity starting with understanding the fundamental legal principle of 'valid consent'.

We will examine some models that are used to understand mental disorder in order to explore notions of power and control. The social perspective on mental distress will be introduced and how social workers can work with the power and authority that is inherent in their role will be explored. However, there is only room for an introduction to these themes, which are worthy of much deeper exploration. There will be suggested further reading for you to explore models of mental disorder in more depth if you so wish.

Throughout this chapter we will be using terminology that was in use at the time these Acts of Parliament were in force. You might find the use of these terms offensive and upsetting but they do give us an insight into the attitudes and social norms of the time. It will become apparent that whilst the terminology has changed, the way that we categorise and label people who are mentally distressed has changed very little. Throughout this book, we will be using the term 'mental disorder' when referring to people who may come within the provisions of mental health legislation. This is because it is a legal term and this is a book about mental health law. As we will see, it is an umbrella term covering a range of people with differing mental disorders including those with mental illnesses, learning disabilities and personality disorders. It is important that social workers do not accept or use these terms and concepts uncritically as these terms are imbued with assumptions and underpinned by values that need to be understood. These terms have quite rightly been subject to sharp critique by those who use mental health services. We will explore this in more detail when we consider models of mental disorder but at times we will use the broader, and hopefully less stigmatising, term 'mental distress'.

The history of the law in dealing with people with mental disorders

Philip Fennell (in Gostin et al., 2010) sets out an excellent and very detailed account of the development of mental health law from 1324 to the present day. This summary draws from his work.

Before 1800

The root of legal intervention in the affairs of people with mental disorders goes back to 1324 when Edward II issued his 'De Prerogative Regis' to deal with the property of 'natural fools' (those who we now would consider to have a learning disability) and 'lunatics' (who we would now say have a mental illness). The first hospital to look after those who were 'lunatics' was Bethlem Hospital, which opened in 1247 but started looking after those with mental disorders in 1377. During the medieval period Bethlem mainly looked after lunatics who were a menace to themselves or others, when there was no one else to keep them safe. The main method of treatment was the use of mechanical restraint and conditions were poor.

We begin to see the development of the welfare state and roots of the social work profession in the Poor Relief Act of 1601. This law was enacted by Elizabeth I and it was left unaltered until 1834. This Act made each parish responsible for supporting the legitimately needy in their community. These deserving poor were: young orphans, the elderly, and the mentally and physically disabled. It is interesting to note that the debate about those who are deserving and not deserving of state benefits has not really moved on at all in the intervening 400 years.

The Vagrancy Act 1744 marks the first appearance of an express statutory power for Justices of the Peace to order the detention and restraint of those who 'by lunacy or otherwise are furiously mad or so disordered in their senses that they may be dangerous to go abroad'. Prior to this there was only the common law power to detain someone to prevent a breach of the peace (a power that still exists). The eighteenth century was a time when, in the absence of state provision, private madhouses began to be opened. At this time there was no legal authority for their existence and there was no regulation.

Whilst we are used to thinking of mental health law as contained in one statute, the law in this area developed in separate streams of statutes throughout the nineteenth century and the beginning of the twentieth. These separate strands of law were only brought together in the Mental Health Act 1959. These strands included:

- The law in relation to private patients.
- The law in relation to 'pauper' lunatics.
- The law in relation to the mentally incapacitated and the 'mentally defective'.
- The law in relation to the 'criminally insane'.

The Madhouses Act of 1774 was the first attempt to regulate the activities of private madhouses. This Act provided legal authority for these madhouses and a rudimentary system of safeguards. Private madhouses had become a byword for wrongful confinement and abuse. Following this Act, in order for confinement in a madhouse to be lawful it had to be in a place authorised by law to detain. Also, for the first time, there had to be medical evidence of 'unsoundness of mind' before confinement could be justified. However, this system was still open to abuse as the Act was not clear on the qualifications that these doctors needed.

1800 to 1900

The County Asylums Act 1808 gave the power to magistrates of each county to establish an asylum, although many did not. Where there were asylums, conditions were often appalling. In 1814 a scandal arose when a magistrate visiting Bethlem Hospital found a side room with ten naked female patients chained to the wall and in a dungeon he discovered James Norris, his body enclosed in a device of iron bars and chained to the trough where he lay. He was kept in this iron harness due to the unusual shape of his hands and wrists. He was considered to be a very dangerous and violent man. He had been confined in this harness for nine years and he died of tuberculosis a few days after his release. Following this scandal, and after two select committee investigations, the Lunacy Commission was set up in 1828, initially covering London, and expanded to the rest of the country in 1842. The role of the Commissioners was to license and inspect madhouses, a role that is still carried out today by the Care Quality Commission and its Mental Health Act reviewers (formerly Mental Health Act commissioners).

Following the Victorian Industrial Revolution there was a need to revise the Elizabethan Poor Law, and the Poor Law Amendment Act 1834 came into force. The system of 'outdoor relief' (money and other benefits to people in their own homes) was phased out in favour of 'indoor relief', i.e. moving people into workhouses. Conditions in workhouses were deliberately harsh to act as a deterrent. Poor Law relieving officers were responsible for distributing this relief.

The Lunatics Act 1845 laid the foundations of the modern English mental health legislation with the establishment of a national network of public asylums. The state became increasingly involved in dealing with the mentally disordered and the asylum was the sole officially approved method of dealing with this problem. With the rise of the medical profession, madness was increasingly being seen as something that could be diagnosed, certified and treated by experts, i.e. doctors (Scull in Fennell, 2010: p13). However, there was an increasing awareness that no effective treatments for madness existed at this time.

Following concerns over the lack of any independent view or judicial oversight regarding the need for a patient to be confined, the Lunacy Act 1890 introduced a requirement that confinement be based on a 'certification' by a judicial authority based on medical certificates. There were separate procedures for pauper lunatics and those who could afford private madhouses. In the case of pauper lunatics, Poor Law relieving officers were responsible for bringing the case to a magistrate after obtaining the required medical certificates. In the case of a private patient, a relative could bring the case before a magistrate. Detention was now for a fixed period of time rather than indefinitely as was previously the case.

1900 to present day

The first major mental health legislation of the twentieth century related to what would today be called people with a learning disability. It was in response to concerns about the 'high rate of propagation of mental defectives' and the threat of 'national degeneration'. The Mental Deficiency Act 1913 was wider in scope than previous Acts, relating to 'idiots' and 'imbeciles' who were not capable of looking after themselves. It enabled 'feeble minded' subjects to be dealt with by the state. Also this Act introduced a new category of 'moral imbecility', which allowed for the detention of many on moral grounds such as having children out of wedlock. Many of these women remained in institutions up to the 1980s until the closure of large long-stay hospitals. Guardianship was also introduced by this Act, which allowed mental defectives to be subject to statutory supervision. Local authorities were required to ensure that their control over the person would 'suffice to prevent the defective from procreating children'.

The Mental Treatment Act 1930 gave birth to the role of the duly authorised officer, which effectively replaced the role of the relieving officer under the 1890 Act. The duly authorised officer could assess the need for patients to be treated under two different Acts. They could make applications for temporary treatment with two medical recommendations. They could also decide if the treatment was urgent and remove the person to hospital for up to three days if they posed a risk to themselves or others. This allowed time to take proceedings under the 1890 Act where they took over the role of the relieving officers. The Mental Treatment Act also responded to concerns about overflowing hospitals by authorising local authorities to set up psychiatric outpatient clinics and to arrange aftercare for patients who had been discharged.

The Percy Commission was set up in 1953 due to human rights concerns following cases of wrongful detention under the Mental Deficiency Act 1913, but according to Fennell (2010: p38) the Government had its own agenda to further medicalise mental health law and take account of the development of the National Health Service in 1948.

This Commission led to the Mental Health Act 1959 which still provides the basic framework of modern English and Welsh mental health law. This Act removed the need for judicial certification. Instead there had to be an application to the hospital by either the nearest relative of the patient or the mental welfare officer supported by two medical recommendations. Learning disability and mental illness were brought under one statute for the first time. There were now four categories of mental disorder. Given the abuses of the 1913 Act no one could be treated as mentally disordered by reason only of promiscuity or other immoral conduct. It is interesting to note that the Mental Health Act 2007 removed this prohibition, presumably to bring paedophiles within the provisions of mental health law. Local health authorities had a duty to appoint sufficient mental welfare officers and these duties were transferred to the new all-purpose social services departments in 1971.

The Mental Health Act 1983 was a much less radical Act than the 1959 Act it replaced and it retains most of its structure and provisions. The approved social worker (ASW) replaced the mental welfare officer. According to Webber (2008: p20), ASWs had extended powers and greater professional autonomy to exercise an independent opinion than their predecessors. They were charged with bringing a social perspective and investigating the possibility of using other services to avoid the need for admission to hospital.

After two failed attempts to introduce a completely new Mental Health Act in 2002 and 2004 due to overwhelming opposition to the public protection ethos of the then Labour Government's proposals, the 1983 Act was amended by the introduction of the Mental Health Act 2007. The system of application for detention was retained. However the role was widened to include nurses, occupational therapists and psychologists, as well as social workers, and renamed the approved mental health professional (AMHP). The four categories of mental disorder left over from 1959 were replaced by a single broader definition of mental disorder. As the 2007 Act was an amending Act, the Mental Health Act 1983 is still in force, albeit significantly changed.

ACTIVITY **2.1**

Why are non-medical professionals involved in the process of detention?

When considering if a person needs to be detained due to their mental disorder, there are now medical and non-medical professionals involved in that decision. Why? What would happen if we left such decisions solely in the hands of medical professionals? What benefits are there in having non-medical professionals involved in the process?

Since the 1959 Act the importance of the social perspective as a counterpoint to the medical perspective has continued to gain ground. This is not just due to the increasing independence of ASWs under the 1983 Act, but more contemporarily with the increasing voice of the service user/survivor movements. Social workers are uniquely placed to hear the views of service users and give weight to them when considering the use of the Mental Health Act 1983 or Mental Capacity Act 2005. There are several safeguards within these two statutes. These safeguards are not safeguards if patients and service users are not able to avail themselves of them. It could be argued that the mental health system is facing huge challenges and is under strain as never before. As a result social workers are uniquely placed to champion the need to uphold the human rights of vulnerable adults who use health and social services.

Mental incapacity and the law

While we can see that law dealing with those who were found to be 'mentally deficient' has a long and chequered history, the notion of mental incapacity is much more recent. As we have already said, the first statute defining mental incapacity was the Mental Capacity Act 2005. However, mental incapacity was defined in case law before this statute came into force. Before we can examine the development of the law around mental incapacity, we need to understand a fundamental principle in UK law with regard to medical treatment and care: the principle of 'valid consent'.

The principle of valid consent

The principle of valid consent is based on the fundamental right of a capable adult to make a decision about what can and cannot be done to their body. This is called patient autonomy and it is well defined and established in case law. Lord Donaldson in (*Re T* [1992] 4 All ER 649) states:

> An adult who . . . suffers from no mental incapacity has an absolute right to choose whether to consent to treatment, to refuse it or to choose one rather than that other

treatment being offered . . . this right of choice is not limited to decisions which others might regard as sensible. It exists notwithstanding that the reasons for making the choice are rational, irrational, unknown or even non-existent. The fact that emergency cases apart, no medical treatment of an adult patient of full capacity can be undertaken without his consent creates a situation in which in the absence of consent has much the same effect as refusal.

The courts have confirmed this fundamental principle time and time again. For a capable adult their consent is required before they can be given medical treatment even when their refusal of treatment could result in their death. If treatment is provided to a capable adult without them giving consent, this may amount to: a civil wrong (trespass to the person), a criminal offence (assault) and violate the person's rights under the European Convention on Human Rights.

So what is consent? This is to be found in case law but we can also find a clearly set out definition in the Mental Health Act Code of Practice (MHA Code) (Department of Health, 2015a):

> Consent is the voluntary and continuing permission of a patient to be given a particular treatment, based on a sufficient knowledge of the purpose, nature, likely effects and risks of that treatment, including the likelihood of its success and any alternatives to it. Permission given under any unfair or undue pressure is not consent.
>
> (para 24.34)

You will note that this definition states that the patient must be given sufficient information. What is sufficient information? This will depend on the needs and wishes of the patient. Doctors have to make a judgement in each particular case of what information to give to their patient. Some patients will want a lot of information about the particular treatment they are considering and others will want less. Doctors should invite the patient to ask questions about the treatment being proposed and provide full, frank and truthful answers (MHA Code, para 24.38). Also, there may be situations where providing too much information may overwhelm the patient, with the result that they may not be able to make a decision at all. The law recognises the duty of doctors to provide 'sufficient' information to their patients without overwhelming them and that this is a matter for professional judgement (*Bolam v Friern Hospital Management Committee* [1957] 2 All ER 118). This system of being provided with sufficient information, based on the doctor's judgement, to enable the patient to make a decision, is called 'valid consent'. It contrasts with other systems of consent operating in other countries, such as in the United States where there is a requirement on doctors to provide much more information about a certain treatment based on what a reasonable patient would want to know. This system is called 'informed consent'. There is considerable debate about which system is to be preferred as some view the UK system to be based on medical paternalism rather than a human-rights-based approach. (See Lord Scarman disagreeing with the majority view, called a dissenting judgment, in *Sidaway v Board of Bethlem Royal Hospital* [1985] 1 All ER 643.)

We can see that the information provided to the patient must include the purpose of the treatment, i.e. what it is trying to achieve; the nature of the treatment, i.e. what the treatment is; what its likely effects (including side effects) are; and what the risks are.

The law around mental incapacity

We now know that medical treatment cannot be given to a capable patient without their consent. What happens if the patient is not capable of giving their consent? Prior to the Mental Capacity Act 2005, common law provided the legal authority to treat a person in their best interests under the doctrine of 'necessity'. However, before the treatment could be provided under this legal doctrine it had to be established that the person lacked the mental capacity to make the decision.

One of the most important cases where the courts set out the correct approach in determining mental capacity was *Re C* (*Re C (adult: refusal of medical treatment)* [1994] 1 All ER 819). C was a 68-year-old man with schizophrenia who was detained in Broadmoor Hospital (a high secure hospital for patients with a mental disorder). His leg became ulcerated and gangrenous. He was transferred to a general hospital where the surgeon advised that he needed to have his leg amputated below the knee otherwise he would die. The patient refused. He wanted the hospital to give an undertaking that the leg would not be amputated at some future date. When they refused he went to court to apply for an injunction preventing the hospital from amputating his leg without his written consent. The case centred on the issue of whether or not he had the capacity to make a decision regarding the treatment of his leg. C suffered from grandiose delusions in that he believed that he was a highly skilled vascular surgeon (he was not), and had paranoid beliefs that whatever medical treatment was offered was calculated to destroy his body. As a result, his consultant psychiatrist at Broadmoor Hospital believed that he lacked capacity to make this decision. However, the court disagreed, finding that there was no direct link between his delusional beliefs and his refusal to consent to the amputation. The court stated that there were three stages to making a decision: taking in and retaining the information; believing the information; and weighing the information, balancing the risks and needs. This became known as the incapacity test and formed the basis of the capacity test in the Mental Capacity Act 2005. In the case of C, Judge Thorpe stated:

> I am completely satisfied that the presumption that C has the right of self-determination has not been displaced. Although his general capacity is impaired by schizophrenia, it has not been established that he does not sufficiently understand the nature, purpose and effects of the treatment he refuses. Indeed, I am satisfied that he has understood and retained the relevant information, that in his own way he believes it, and that in the same fashion he has arrived at a clear choice.

The patient obtained the injunction preventing his leg being amputated and he did not die (from his gangrenous leg). This case also established in law the principle that a valid and applicable advance decision to refuse treatment made by a patient must be followed even when the patient later lacks the capacity to make this decision. Advance decisions will be discussed in more detail in Chapter 6.

It is important to note that this case was based on the principle in UK law that the patient requires 'sufficient' information regarding the medical treatment being proposed in that the court determined that C was able to sufficiently understand the information. If we had a system of informed consent where the patient needs to understand all the material information, it may be that C being able to sufficiently understand the information would not have been enough. One of the implications of this system of 'valid consent' for social workers is that they may need to work with doctors to enable them to provide information to service users in such a manner that maximises the chances of the service user being able to sufficiently understand the information provided.

ACTIVITY *2.2*

Obtaining valid consent

Imagine you are having a discussion with your general practitioner about a physical health problem you have that requires an operation. Think about what information you will need about your condition and the operation before you can make a decision. In what form do you want this information and how can your doctor help you with this? Is there a situation where you can have too much information, or where information is presented in such a way that it makes it more difficult for you to make a decision?

Now think about a vulnerable adult that you are working with who faces the same decision. How would you support them to gather and understand the information they need to make a decision? Would the information need to be presented differently and how much detail would they need?

Models of mental disorder

As we shall see there are a range of different ways to understand and conceptualise mental disorder or mental distress. It is important that you have some understanding of these models of mental disorder, as they will not only inform your practice in working with adults experiencing mental distress; you will also become aware of the models that shape the approaches of other professionals you will be working with, such as psychiatrists, mental health nurses, psychologists and advocates.

Medical model

The medical model is sometimes called the biological model. Dallos (in Heller et al., 1996) states that frameworks that draw on biological explanations see mental distress as resulting from mainly physical causes. That mental distress results from hereditary factors, damage to the body or defects in the brain, e.g. defects in the neurotransmitters which carry signals around the brain. The medical model sees mental disorders in much the same way as physical disorders, in that they can be diagnosed in terms of definable syndromes, or clusters of symptoms, and given a name or label. Once a name or label has been allocated to the group of symptoms by the expert (the psychiatrist) a treatment is prescribed (usually medication) in much the same way that physical disorders are treated.

This model has been subject to much critique, not just from patients, service users and survivors as we shall see below, but also from within the psychiatric profession. Bentall (2003: p152) discusses Szasz's view that once a person has been diagnosed as 'mentally ill' such individuals can be coerced into undergoing 'treatment' so that they will conform more fully to social norms. Szasz described mental health professionals as belonging to a kind of police force that controls and limits the amount of deviance within society. This concern that psychiatry can be used as a form of social control can been seen in the reaction to human rights abuses following the Mental Deficiency Act 1913, when women were detained for getting pregnant outside of marriage. More recently the medical model has been subject to critique from lesbian and gay perspectives as well as from those from Black and Minority Ethnic communities.

Despite this critique, the medical model is still a very powerful model within mental health because as Rogers and Pilgrim (2010: p2) argue, 'the illness framework is the dominant framework in mental health services because psychiatry is the dominant profession within those services'. They do go on to say that the illness framework has its strengths in terms of its logic and empirical status, but that the fundamental problem with this approach is that the judgements made about whether a person is mentally ill or not focus mainly on what the person is able to communicate about the symptoms they are experiencing, rather than finding any physical changes in the body or brain.

However, there are those from within the psychiatric profession who argue for a broader biopsychological approach, which accepts that mental illnesses have primarily psychological and social causes, and that context is of essential importance in the understanding of mental health problems (Double, 2005: p56). In trying to understand the relevance of context we need to explore alternative approaches to mental disorder.

Social models

Any exploration of social perspectives on mental disorder will lead to the conclusion that, unlike the medical model, it cannot really be understood as a single model. In order to understand the social model of mental disorder we will have to examine a range of perspectives. However, what these perspectives have in common is the understanding that the social context of the person is key to understanding mental distress. Brown (2009: p7) argues that mental illness could be seen as a consequence of social disadvantage, the symptom of a sick society, and that the solution would lie in improving social and physical conditions. As Tew (2005: p13) states, this was recognised by the previous Labour Government through its National Service Framework for Mental Health (Department of Health, 1999) as well as its social inclusion agenda (Office of the Deputy Prime Minister, 2004). However, he argues that there is nothing really new in the social model of mental distress as it has long been on the agenda of areas such as sociology, psychology, social work, family therapy, transcultural psychiatry, the women's movement, the lesbian and gay movements, the disability movement, mental health service user networks and the recovery movement.

Tew (2005: p16) sets out what he sees as the strengths of the social model. The social model must not be reduced to a single model as there is a need for a plurality of overlapping perspectives that reflect the complexity and diversity of experience based on a range of factors including: gender, culture, economic status, age, family and personal relationships. However, he argues, this does not mean that the social model cannot have at its core a set of values that are fundamental. The social model argues for the end of the 'us' and 'them' thinking which decides who is 'normal' and who is 'abnormal'. This would see mental distress as part of a continuum of everyday lived experience. It would also mean that people who are experiencing mental distress would be understood in terms of their social context rather than just in terms of signs and symptoms. A social model has to take seriously and hear what people are saying about their mental distress, as well as the histories, meanings and aspirations they attach to them. Any social perspective needs to be informed by the principles of anti-oppressive practice, which requires an awareness of power differentials between professionals and those who use services as well as addressing issues such as stigma, discrimination and inequality.

Tew (2005: p17) argues that the social model should move away from evidence-based practice as this knowledge is gathered in a way which assumes a uniformity of experience and seeks to give professionals tools to treat people as passive subjects. However, this view is not universal within the social model. The strength of the medical model is seen in its empirical framework, which is best practice based on evidence of what works and what does not. There are social work academics and researchers like Martin Webber (2008: p1) who argue that as social workers are increasingly working in multi-disciplinary teams, they are increasingly called on to justify their practice to health colleagues whose training is based on evidence from empirical research. He states that without this, social work could be perceived as lacking in credibility as it struggles to articulate its evidence base. More latterly he has been involved in developing the evidence base for social work interventions in mental health such as the Connecting People Intervention Study (**www.connectingpeoplestudy.net**) (Webber, 2014).

No examination of social models on mental distress would be complete without at least a cursory glance at those perspectives that arise from groups such as women, Black and Minority Ethnic communities, and lesbian and gay communities. We have already touched on the notion of psychiatry as an agent of social control. This still has a powerful effect on these groups within society today and it is important that these effects are explored and understood.

An overview of research into Black people in the mental health system highlights some key issues (Ferns, 2005: p130). There is an over-representation of Black people within the psychiatric system and these are more likely to come into the system via being detained under the Mental Health Act 1983. There is a lack of preventative and aftercare services which are appropriate for Black and Minority Ethnic communities. There is an overuse of drugs and physical treatments (such as electroconvulsive therapy) with Black service users rather than talking therapies. Black people are more likely to be diagnosed with psychosis and more likely to be labelled as 'dangerous'. Some of the key themes that Ferns (2005: p138) draws out include oppression as well as the use of power and authority. He argues that there are two types of authority that are applied to Black people: protective authority and oppressive authority (Ferns, 2005: p140). Protective authority is described as where practitioners (including social workers) act with vulnerable people to safeguard their interests and reduce unnecessary risks to them and/or others within a legislative framework that protects their rights. Oppressive authority is where practitioners act consciously or unconsciously to uphold a discriminatory approach to society and a dominating style of professional practice, which seeks to contain, suppress and coerce individuals or social groups. If we are considering social work intervention with Black mental health service users, we can see that we need to be especially alert to the issues of power and oppression and seek to use the Mental Health Act 1983 and Mental Capacity Act 2005 in a way which embodies the principles of protective authority.

When we go on to consider the impact of mental health services on women we also have to consider issues of power and inequality. Williams (2005: p151) argues that it is valid and useful to conceptualise women's mental health problems as responses to damaging experiences that are rooted in their lived experiences of inequality and abuses of power. For her the key to understanding women's mental distress is to understand the social context in which many women live their lives. She argues that the efficacy of mental health services rests on their capacity to provide respectful and safe relationships within which women can tell their own stories of disempowerment and survival (Williams, 2005: p164).

While notions of power are important when we consider the position of lesbians and gay men within the mental health system, we need to consider the universality of the oppression that lesbians and gay men have faced. Barbara Gittings, one of the founders of the US gay liberation movement during the late 1950s, powerfully states:

> Psychiatrists were one of the three major groups that had their hands on us. Religion and the law were the other two. So besides being sick we were sinful and criminal. But the sickness label infected everything we said and made it difficult to gain any credibility for anything we said for ourselves. The sickness label was paramount.
>
> (Quoted in Carr, 2005: p172)

Whilst being Black or a woman was not ever considered to be a mental disorder, being gay was. Homosexuality was classified as a mental disorder until the publication of the tenth edition of the World Health Organisation's International Classification of Diseases in 1992. Psychiatry and psychotherapy has a shameful history of trying to 'convert' homosexuals into heterosexuals using barbaric techniques such as aversion therapy involving use of vomit inducing drugs and electric shocks (Carr, 2005: p172). Sex between two men was decriminalised in 1967 and then after that only if you were over 21. An equal age of consent was only achieved in 2000. It would be tempting to think that with the legalisation of same-sex marriage in 2014, we can put these issues behind us. We have had legal equality for women and Black people for many years but there will be few people who will argue that these groups have achieved full equality, and the same is true for lesbians and gay men. Studies show that lesbians, bisexuals and gay men are at greater risk of psychological problems and that lesbians and gay men are higher users of mental health services than heterosexuals (King and McKeown, 2003: p49).

Service user perspectives

The rise of the service user movement may be considered a relatively new phenomenon. However, its roots can be traced at least as far back as 1845 when John Perceval set up the Alleged Lunatics' Friend Society in 1845 (Wise, 2012: p79). (John Perceval was the son of Spencer Perceval, the Prime Minister who was assassinated in 1812 when he was shot in the House of Commons.)

Service user perspectives challenge the dominance of the medical model and in some cases wider professional intervention. Beresford (2005: p36) states:

> Other professions like social work have sought to inject wider social understandings into their professional approach and understanding. But generally these have taken as given the over-arching medicalised framework of 'mental illness', although differing in the extent to which they saw it as a consequence of nature or nurture.

He goes on to state that user involvement has become one of the guiding formal principles of mental health policy, and that this means we should be hearing from other voices and accessing different viewpoints and understandings. However, in his view, the dominant medical model of understanding mental distress has been internalised by service users. He argues for a new, survivor-led understanding of madness and distress developed by people trying to make sense of their own experience by sharing, collecting and analysing (Beresford, 2005: pp37–44).

We can see that even within the social model of mental distress, there is not one singular approach that social workers can adopt. This is an area where you need to be clear about your own value base as a social worker for this will shape the fundamental assumptions you make when dealing with people who are experiencing mental distress. If you approach this area of work without a clear understanding of what drives you as a social worker, you run the risk of using the authority that comes from your position oppressively rather than using protective authority to ultimately promote independence and recovery in those with whom you work. This is something we explore in the following case study.

CASE STUDY

Jacek

Jacek is an east-European man in his 20s. He has been in the UK for two years and works as a barber in town. He lives in a shared house with other European Union nationals. He has family in his home country, who he helps to support financially. He gets paid the minimum wage and works long hours in order to be able to afford to live and send money home. He has struggled to make friends locally and he is using cannabis to help him relax. He has a history of depression, which started in his teens. However, more recently his workmates have reported that he has been acting strangely. He has taken apart the electric sockets at work because he believes that bugs have been placed in them. He keeps talking about a former workmate who he believes is spying on him through cameras and drones. His boss at work is very worried about him and has been trying to get Jacek to see his GP.

Think about the models of mental disorder we have discussed and consider how the medical model would seek to understand Jacek's mental distress. What approach would be taken for Jacek and how would his problems be formulated? What approach would the medical model take in trying to address what is happening to him?

CHAPTER SUMMARY

- Mental health law has been evolving since the mid-eighteenth century and parallels the rise of the medical profession and its increasing involvement in dealing with people who experience mental distress.

- There has been increasing non-medical involvement in mental health law to counter the power of medical professionals.

- The current Mental Health Act has now been in force for over 30 years, although it has been subject to various amendments over that time.

- The principle of valid consent is based on the fundamental right of a capable adult to make a decision about what can and cannot be done to their body.

- The law around people who lack capacity to make certain decisions developed through case law which was mostly incorporated into the Mental Capacity Act 2005.

- Social workers need to be aware of a range of models of mental disorder that challenge the dominance of the medical model.

Tew, J (ed) (2005) *Social Perspectives in Mental Health.* London: Jessica Kingsley.

This is a useful book which explores different ways of understanding and approaching mental distress.

Wise, S (2012) *Inconvenient People: Lunacy, Liberty and Mad-Doctors in Victorian England.* London: The Bodley Head.

A book written by a historian about the abuses of the mental health system in Victorian England. It has some very interesting insights into the medical profession and the development of the law around mentally disordered people.

Chapter 3

Introduction to the Mental Health Act 1983 and Mental Capacity Act 2005

Introduction

In this chapter we start to look at mental health law in more detail. We will start to examine the two key statutes which will underpin the work of social workers and other professionals in this area of law: the Mental Health Act 1983 (MHA) and the Mental Capacity Act 2005 (MCA). Both these Acts have been amended by the Mental

Health Act 2007. In order for you to even begin to grasp the sometimes complex provisions of these two pieces of legislation, it is important that you understand what these Acts set out to achieve, i.e. what their purpose is. If you cannot understand their purpose, then you will struggle to understand how these Acts apply to your work and how their provisions will apply to the service users with whom you are working, and you run the risk of acting unlawfully.

The Mental Health Act starts out, rather unsurprisingly, by setting out what is and is not a mental disorder. The Mental Capacity Act, in its early sections, defines mental incapacity. This chapter will introduce these two key concepts and seek to apply them to social work tasks. There is statutory guidance available to social workers to enable them to understand and use these Acts in their work. The chapter will introduce the three Codes of Practice: Mental Health Act Code of Practice (Department of Health, 2015a), Mental Capacity Act Code of Practice (Department of Constitutional Affairs, 2007) and the supplement to the MCA Code which covers Deprivation of Liberty Safeguards (Ministry of Justice, 2008). It is expected that social workers will have access to these three Codes and be familiar with their contents. The chapter will end with an examination of key roles within these two Acts and set out some commonly used terms and abbreviations.

The purpose of the Mental Health Act

As we have seen from previous chapters, the current MHA is the development of a long series of Acts of Parliament that attempt to address the care and treatment of people with a mental disorder. Section 1(1) of the MHA sets out the purpose of the Act:

> The provisions of this Act shall have effect with respect to the reception, care and treatment of mentally disordered patients, the management of their property and other related matters.

Brown et al. (2009: p9) state that this Act provides for both informal and compulsory care and treatment of people who have a mental disorder. Informal care is care that is provided without use of compulsion under this Act. Section 131 states that nothing in this Act should prevent a patient who requires treatment for mental disorder from being admitted to any hospital without being detained. The courts have expounded on the purpose of this Act stating that the policy and objectives of the Act are to:

> regulate the circumstances in which the liberty of persons who are mentally disordered may be restricted and, where there is conflict, to balance their interests against those of public policy.

(Jones, 2013: 1–004)

Clearly the focus of this Act is with people (called patients in this Act) who are mentally disordered. If a person is not, or in some cases does not appear to be, mentally disordered then this Act does not apply to them. Therefore, we can understand that the purpose of this Act is to do with the treatment of people who have a mental disorder and provides for the state to deprive them of or restrict their liberty in certain circumstances.

This leads us to consider what liberty is. The Human Rights Act 1998 (HRA) came into effect in the United Kingdom in October 2000. However, the purpose of this Act was not to provide any new 'human rights' as the UK has been a signatory to the European Convention on Human Rights (ECHR) since the early 1950s. Its purpose was to incorporate certain Convention rights (called Articles) into UK law. HRA section 6(1) states 'it is unlawful for a public authority to act in a way which is incompatible with a Convention right'. While 'public authority' is not defined under the Act, it includes anyone who is a carrying out a function of a public nature. This will include health and social care professionals, and therefore social workers are subject to the provisions of the Human Rights Act. A full exploration of the ECHR is beyond the scope of this book. However, at this point we need to be familiar with Article 5 of the Convention as it pertains to the liberty and security of the person. We will discuss other Convention rights as we come across them. Article 5 states:

> Everyone has the right to liberty and security of person. No one should be deprived of his liberty save in the following cases and in accordance with a procedure prescribed by law . . . the lawful detention of . . . persons of unsound mind.

> Everyone who is deprived of his liberty by arrest or detention shall be entitled to take proceedings by which the lawfulness of his detention shall be decided speedily by a court and his release ordered if the detention is not lawful.

We can see that the right to liberty and security of person is not absolute, i.e. it can be interfered with by the state in specific cases. There are certain Convention rights that are absolute (such as Article 3 which provides for the prohibition of torture) but most of them are 'qualified' which means they can be interfered with by the state in certain circumstances. In the case of people with a mental disorder, they have to be mentally disordered (or in some cases at least appear to be mentally disordered) and 'a procedure prescribed by law' has to be applied to them. The Mental Health Act 1983 fulfils the UK's obligations under the Convention to have a procedure prescribed by law with respect of the detention of people of 'unsound mind'.

We can see that the primary purpose of the Mental Health Act is to provide a lawful mechanism by which people who are considered to be mentally disordered can be subject to restrictions on their liberty in certain cases in order to provide them with care and treatment. It does this by providing procedures for admitting patients to hospital, provision for the use of compulsion in the community, provisions for the treatment of mentally disordered people concerned in criminal proceedings, provisions for providing medical treatment and other related provisions.

The purpose of the Mental Capacity Act

Unlike the MHA, the MCA is not the latest of a long series of Acts dealing with issues around mental capacity and incapacity. As we have previously discussed, this Act brings into statute provisions that already existed under the common law doctrine of 'necessity'. The preamble to the Act states quite simply that this is 'an Act to make new provision relating to persons who lack capacity'. Lord Falconer in his introduction to the MCA Code of Practice states that the Act is:

> a vitally important piece of legislation, and one that will make a real difference to the lives of people who may lack mental capacity. It will empower people to make decisions for themselves wherever possible, and protect people who lack capacity by providing a flexible framework that places individuals at the very heart of the decision-making process. It will ensure that they participate as much as possible in any decisions made on their behalf, and that these are made in their best interests.

We can see that this Act is primarily concerned with people who do not have the mental capacity to make certain decisions. If there is no suggestion that a person lacks mental capacity to make the decisions in question then this Act will not apply. There are some exceptions to this rule (such as the ability for a person to plan ahead to a time in the future when they may lack capacity), but on the whole the Act is solely concerned with people who have been found to lack mental capacity at least for some decisions that they need to make. It is important to note that social workers are more likely to need recourse to the provisions of this Act, rather than the MHA. As Jones (2012: 1–002) states, the MCA:

> is a measure which is likely to touch the lives of everyone because, at some point, all adults will probably be affected by a lack of capacity to make decisions relating to their everyday lives, either personally, or though contact with people who are unable to make decisions for themselves.

The provisions of the MCA intrude on that most private of spaces, a person's autonomy. That is, as we have already discussed in Chapter 2:

> An adult who . . . suffers from no mental incapacity has an absolute right to choose whether to consent to treatment, to refuse it or to choose one rather than another treatment being offered . . . this right of choice is not limited to decisions which others might regard as sensible. It exists not withstanding that the reasons for making the choice are rational, irrational, unknown or even non-existent. The fact that emergency cases apart, no medical treatment of an adult patient of full capacity can be undertaken without his consent, creates a situation in which the absence of consent has much the same effect as refusal.

> (Lord Donaldson in *Re T* [1992] 4 All ER 649)

As the MCA can potentially interfere with this normally private and personal domain, we need to go back to the European Convention on Human Rights to see what it may have to say about the state interfering with a person's private life. Article 8 of the Convention provides for the right to respect for private and family life:

> Everyone has the right to respect for his private and family life, his home and his correspondence. There shall be no interference by a public authority with the exercise

of this right except such as is in accordance with the law and is necessary in a democratic society in the interests of national security, public safety or the economic well-being of the country, for the prevention of disorder or crime, for the protection of health or morals, or the protection of the rights and freedoms of others.

As we can see, as with Article 5, the right to respect for private and family life is a qualified right and can be interfered with by the state in certain circumstances. In order for this interference to be lawful, it has to be 'in accordance with the law' and necessary (in the case of MCA) for the protection of health.

We can see that the purpose of the MCA is to provide for decisions to be made in respect of people who do not have the mental capacity to make those decisions for themselves. Without this Act these decisions would be unlawful as they either would amount to an assault on the person or they would interfere with the person's right to a private and family life. The Act sets out what mental capacity is and provides for decisions to be made in a person's best interests; for Lasting Powers of Attorney, for the appointment of deputies, for the making of advance decisions, for provision of independent mental capacity advocates, and sets out the powers available to the Court of Protection and the Deprivation of Liberty Safeguards.

ACTIVITY **3.1**

Which Act applies?

Consider the following situations and decide which of the Mental Health Act or the Mental Capacity Act applies:

1. *A young man who is presenting with psychotic symptoms is refusing treatment in the community and needs to be admitted to hospital.*

2. *A woman with a moderate learning disability has fallen and broken her leg. She does not understand the need to go to hospital for treatment and thinks her mother can make the pain go away.*

3. *A young man with autism is standing by a lake. He has fascinated by water but cannot swim and does not realise he might drown if he jumps in. You are concerned that he might jump in the water but he is refusing to come with you back to where he lives.*

4. *A woman has been diagnosed with depression but is so unwell that she is not able to make a decision about taking medication. However, when her husband gives her the medication to take, she takes it and swallows it with a glass of water.*

5. *An older woman with dementia needs to go into hospital for an assessment. She is settled and content. She is not able to make a decision about admission to hospital but does not resist when the ambulance arrives to take her.*

(Continued)

ACTIVITY **3.1** *Continued*

Answers

1. *He needs treatment for a mental disorder in hospital. He is refusing treatment so the Mental Health Act applies.*

2. *The woman has a mental disorder which impacts on her ability to make a decision about her broken leg. The treatment required is not for a mental disorder but a physical one so the Mental Capacity Act applies.*

3. *While there is a mental disorder, the need here is not for assessment or for assessment/treatment in hospital so the Mental Health Act does not apply and the Mental Capacity Act can be used to return him home.*

4. *We are talking about treatment for a mental disorder here, but not in hospital, so the Mental Capacity Act applies.*

5. *Potentially both Acts can apply in this case. The Mental Capacity Act can be used to provide treatment for a mental disorder in hospital if the person lacks capacity to make this decision (as long as there is no deprivation of liberty). However, the Mental Health Act will need to be used if she resists admission to hospital. In some restricted circumstances the Deprivation of Liberty Safeguards may be used (see Chapter 9).*

The definition of mental disorder

As we have seen, the Mental Health Act 1983 only applies to people who are believed to have a mental disorder. In the last chapter we discussed the development of a range of models of mental disorder and we can see that the notion of mental disorder is one that is still subject to considerable debate. However, we need to examine the legal definition of mental disorder in order to understand who the MHA applies to and who it does not.

The Mental Health Act 2007 amended the definition of mental disorder in section 1 of the 1983 Act to give a broad definition. Section 1(2) describes mental disorder as 'any disorder or disability of the mind'.

It could be argued that this is a remarkably simple definition for what we have seen is a complex issue. Jones (2013: 1–024) states the Government's rationale for this change was that they wanted to replace the previous four classifications of mental disorder with one simpler definition under which a patient's needs and risk, not the label that happens to be applied to a mental disorder, determine what action is taken. The Government argued that a single simple definition would also make the Act easier for clinicians to use and for others to understand.

It is important to note that this definition talks about disorders of the mind rather than disorders of the mind and/or brain. The Explanatory Notes to the MHA (para 17) state that disorders or disabilities of the brain are not to be considered mental disorders unless they cause or lead to a disability or disorder of the mind as well. Jones

(2013: 1–024) explains that there is no legal definition as to what is the difference between disorder of the brain and disorder of the mind and that this is a matter for clinical judgement.

It is difficult from this definition to work out what is a mental disorder and what is not. Hale (2010: p50) very helpfully attempts to illuminate this definition, stating:

> As ordinary words of the English language, these are wide enough to cover any mental condition which deviates sufficiently from the supposed norm to be thought abnormal and sufficiently deleterious . . . to be termed a disorder or disability.

She goes on to state that a mental disorder is a condition of the mind that has been recognised and described by psychiatrists in one or both of the internationally accepted classifications of mental disorders. These are the World Health Organisation's International Classification of Diseases (ICD–10, 1992) or the American Psychiatric Association's Diagnostic and Statistical Manual of Mental Disorders (DSM–5, 2013). Therefore, we can see that a mental disorder is something that is defined and diagnosed by doctors. This does give some people cause for concern especially given the history of psychiatry's role in oppressive regimes such as the former Soviet Union (British Medical Association, 1992: p66) and psychiatry's attempt to change sexual orientation in lesbian, gay and bisexual people (Davis and Neal, 1996: p17). However, the MHA Code of Practice (para 2.8) makes clear:

> Difference should not be confused with disorder. No-one may be considered to be mentally disordered solely because of their political, religious or cultural beliefs, values or opinions, unless there are proper clinical grounds to believe that they are the symptoms or manifestations of a disability or disorder of the mind. The same is true of a person's involvement, or likely involvement, in illegal, anti-social or 'immoral' behaviour. Beliefs, behaviours or actions which do not result from a disorder or disability of the mind are not a basis for compulsory measures under the Act, even if they appear unusual or cause other people alarm, distress or danger.

Hale (2010: p41) warns that 'psychiatry is not an exact science. Diagnosis is not easy or clear cut'. The MHA Code (para 2.7) explains the importance of doctors taking care in reaching a diagnosis:

> Care must always be taken to avoid diagnosing, or failing to diagnose, mental disorder on the basis of preconceptions about people or failure to appreciate cultural and social differences. What may be indicative of mental disorder in one person, given their background and individual circumstances, may be nothing of the sort in another person.

The MHA Code (para 2.5) does set out a list of possible mental disorders which includes:

- affective disorders such as depression and bipolar disorder
- schizophrenia and delusional disorders
- neurotic, stress-related and somatoform disorders, such as anxiety, phobic disorders, obsessive compulsive disorder, post-traumatic stress disorder and hypochondriacal disorders

- organic mental disorders such as dementia and delirium (however caused)
- personality and behavioural changes caused by brain injury or damage
- personality disorders
- mental and behavioural disorders caused by psychoactive substance use
- eating disorders, non-organic sleep disorders and non-organic sexual disorders
- learning disabilities
- autistic spectrum disorders
- behavioural and emotional disorders of children and young people

Despite this very broad definition of mental disorder, there are a number of exclusions to what can be legally considered a mental disorder.

Section 1(3) of the Act states that dependence on alcohol or drugs alone is not to be considered to be a mental disorder. As Jones (2013: 1–027) states this is rather an odd exclusion because both dependence on drugs and alcohol are defined as mental disorders in both international classifications of mental disorders discussed above. However, as the MHA Code (paras 2.11, 2.12) states, alcohol or drug dependence may be accompanied by, or associated with, a mental disorder that does fall within the Act's definition. Also the Act does not exclude other disorders or disabilities of the mind related to the use of drugs or alcohol. These may include withdrawal states that manifest themselves as mental disorder. Therefore, it is possible for people with drug and alcohol dependence to come under the provisions of the MHA, as long as there is also a mental disorder, whether it is related to the drug or alcohol dependence or not. However, they cannot be considered to be mentally disordered just because of the drug or alcohol dependence on its own.

While a learning disability is considered a mental disorder there are some specific conditions that need to be met before anyone with a learning disability can be detained under some longer-term sections of the MHA. Learning disability is defined in section 1(4) of the MHA as a 'state of arrested or incomplete development of the mind which includes significant impairment of intelligence and social functioning'. Please note that as the Act defines learning disability to be 'arrested or incomplete development of the mind', this excludes people whose learning disability derives from an accident, illness or injury that occurred once their mind had fully developed. A brain injury is a disorder of the brain (as opposed to a disorder of the mind). However, as disorders of the brain can result in disorders of the mind a person with a brain injury could come within the provisions of the MHA as long as the criteria are met. MHA section 1(2) states that, for the purposes of some longer-term sections, a learning disability is not a mental disorder unless it is 'associated with abnormally aggressive or seriously irresponsible conduct'. It is important to note that the learning disability has to be 'associated with' the conduct in question. If the abnormally aggressive or seriously irresponsible conduct is associated with some other factor, such as use of alcohol or drugs, then the learning disability is not associated with that conduct. However, if the person with a learning disability has another mental disorder as well, such as bipolar disorder or psychosis, then they could be detained under the longer-term provisions of the MHA as long as the primary need for the treatment was for the mental disorder and not the learning disability. The MHA Code (paras 2.15, 2.16) states:

> Someone with a learning disability and no other form of mental disorder may not be detained for treatment or made subject to guardianship or community treatment order unless their learning disability is accompanied by abnormally aggressive or seriously irresponsible conduct on their part.

> This 'learning disability qualification' applies only to specific sections of the Act. In particular, it does not apply to detention for assessment under section 2 of the Act.

Various commentators have pointed out the difficulties in defining what behaviour may be 'seriously irresponsible' and what aggression is 'abnormal'. Ultimately this is a matter for the courts (and Mental Health Tribunals) to decide. However, the MHA Code (para 20.9) does attempt to shed some light on this issue:

> Neither term is defined in the Act, and it is not possible to define exactly what kind of behaviour would fall into either category. Inevitably, it will depend on the nature of the behaviour and the circumstances in which it is exhibited, and also on the extent to which that conduct gives rise to a serious risk to the health or safety of the patient or to the health or safety of other people, or both.

The MHA Code goes on to list factors that professionals will have to consider before deciding if a person's learning disability is associated with abnormally aggressive or seriously irresponsible conduct. If you work with people with a learning disability then it would be good practice to make sure that you are familiar with the contents of Chapter 20 of the MHA Code.

As Hale (2010: p53) points out the provisions of guardianship under the MHA are not available for the vast majority of people with a learning disability because of the learning disability qualification. Many professionals feel that guardianship is a provision that could benefit people with a learning disability who are subject to exploitation or neglect (Brown, 2009: p11).

CASE STUDY

Jayne

Jayne is in her mid 40s and lives with her wife, Theresa. They were in a civil partnership for ten years before converting it to a marriage this year. Jayne admits that she drinks more than she should. She puts this down to stress at work. Theresa would like Jayne to get help with her drinking and her stress-related problems.

(Continued)

CASE STUDY *Continued*

Is drinking more than the recommended limits a mental disorder? What about her stress-related problems?

Theresa is a spiritualist and attends a local spiritualist group. She believes that she can hear spirits speaking to her and she believes that she is a medium. Jayne is an atheist and thinks that Theresa's beliefs are irrational, that hearing spirits are symptoms of a mental disorder, and that she needs help.

Is hearing spirits speaking evidence of a mental disorder?

COMMENT

Dependence on alcohol alone is not a mental disorder, never mind just drinking more than you should. Stress-related problems could amount to a mental disorder if stress manifested itself in increased anxiety and problems with mood etc. However, just because someone has a mental disorder as defined in MHA section 1, it does not mean that they will automatically meet the legal criteria to be detained in hospital. People with mild to moderate mental disorders are unlikely to be admitted to hospital and much more likely to be treated in the community.

What is a mental disorder or not has to be understood in the context of the person's culture and social experiences. Theresa is not alone in holding these beliefs and these beliefs are consistent with a recognised body of belief. No one should be considered mentally disordered solely because of their religious or cultural beliefs.

The definition of mental capacity

As we have already seen, the legal concept of what constitutes the mental capacity that a person requires to make decisions around medical treatment or care has long been defined in case law. The Mental Capacity Act 2005 has now incorporated this common law definition of mental capacity into statute.

MCA section 2(1) defines people who lack capacity:

> For the purposes of this Act, a person lacks capacity in relation to a matter if at the material time he is unable to make a decision for himself in relation to the matter because of an impairment of, or a disturbance in the functioning of the mind or brain.

The Act goes on to state that this impairment or disturbance can be either permanent or temporary. It is important to note that while on the face of it the definition of mental capacity looks similar to the definition of mental disorder in MHA section 1, they are quite different. A person with a mental disorder will often retain the capacity to make decisions about their treatment or care and a person without a mental disorder may lack the capacity to make care and treatment decisions. The two do not necessarily follow each other and it is important that professionals do not make presumptions about a person's ability to make decisions based on whether they have a mental disorder or not. The definition of mental capacity is much wider than that for mental disorder in several respects. The definition of mental disorder relates to the mind alone whilst for mental capacity it includes the brain as well as the mind. Mental disorder relates to a disorder or disability which is diagnosed by doctors, whilst mental capacity has the lower test of impairment or disturbance which does not need to be permanent or even long lasting at all. As we shall see, mental incapacity does not need to be found by 'objective medical expertise' (*Winterwerp v Netherlands* [1979] 2 EHHR 387) but has to be assessed by the professional who is concerned with the decision in question. Mental disorder is status-based in that there has to be a diagnosis by a registered medical practitioner before the person can come within most of the provisions of the Mental Health Act. Mental capacity relates to the ability of a person to make a specific decision and as a result the MCA is considered to be a piece of law which is functional rather than status-based.

Before we go on to consider how professionals are to assess mental capacity, there are a couple of other points to note when considering the definition of mental capacity. The assessment of capacity has to relate to a specific decision at a specific point in time. It is not correct for a professional to state that a person lacks capacity as a general statement. It is possible that if a person lacks the capacity to make a specific decision, e.g. to take medication for dementia, he or she will retain the capacity to make other decisions, e.g. what to clothes to wear, or what food to eat. Therefore, any assessment of capacity has to relate to a specific decision at the time the person is required to make it. An 'impairment' or 'disturbance' can include conditions such as dementia, learning disability or brain injury, which can have long-lasting effects, or it could include unconsciousness or confusion due to an accident, infection, disease or substance use.

Just because a person has an 'impairment of, or a disturbance in the functioning of the mind or brain' it does not automatically follow that they lack the capacity to make decisions regarding their treatment or care. So the Act, in effect, introduces what has been called a two-staged approach (Brown et al., 2009: p6) to assessing capacity. We have considered the first stage, which has been called the diagnostic test. Section 3 of the Act introduces the second part of the capacity test in what has been called the 'functional test'. In order to assess if the impairment or disturbance means that the person is unable to make the decision in question at the time in question the professional will need to apply the section 3 test which is:

A person is unable to make a decision for himself if he is unable –

(a) to understand the information relevant to the decision,

(b) to retain that information,

(c) to use or weigh t hat information as part of the process of making the decision, or

(d) to communicate his decision (whether by talking, using sign language or any other means).

If the person is not able to do any one of these things then they lack the capacity to make the specific decision at the specific time.

We now need to consider these four elements of the capacity test in more detail. Chapter 4 of the MCA Code of Practice provides very detailed guidance on these four elements which enables professionals to understand how to carry out a test of mental capacity.

Understanding the information

It is important that social workers carefully consider how they will provide the information in relation to the decision. They need to make every effort to provide the information in a way and in a form that will maximise the ability of the person receiving this information to understand it. The information has to be relevant to the decision so it is important to be careful not to overwhelm the person with information to the point where they cannot make the decision at all. Also, the information has to be explained using the most effective form of communication for that person such as: their native language, simple language, sign language, visual cues, symbols etc. The MCA Code defines the relevant information as being relevant to:

- The nature of the decision
- The reason why the decision is needed, and
- The likely effects of deciding one way or another, or making no decision at all.

(para 4.16)

Retaining the information

The requirement is that the person must be able to hold the information in their mind long enough to use to make the decision in question. It is important that professionals do not assume that just because a person can only retain the information for a short time that they lack capacity to make the decision. The test here is, can the person retain the information long enough to make the decision and communicate it. Obviously, the more serious the decision and the more complex the information required, the longer the person will need to retain the information in order to use it in the process of their decision making. The MCA Code of Practice (para 4.2) suggests that items such as notebooks, photographs, posters, videos and voice recorders can help people retain information.

Using or weighing the information

This is often the test that professionals find most difficult to assess and rather unhelpfully the MCA Code of Practice does not have much to say here. This test relates to the person's ability to consider the information given to them and weigh up that information in order to make their decision. For example, if the decision in question is around taking medication for a psychotic disorder but the person does not believe that they have this disorder, the professional assessing their capacity to make this decision may decide that they are not able to use the information about their diagnosis because they are not able to give any weight to their diagnosis of mental disorder.

The MCA Code of Practice (para 4.22) does cite the example of a person with an eating disorder who may understand the information about the consequences of not eating but the compulsion not to eat might be too strong for them to ignore.

Communicating the decision

There are very few people who will not be able to communicate at all (such as people who are unconscious, in a coma or persistent vegetative state). So most people will be able pass this element of the test. It is important for the professional to make all practical steps to help the person communicate. Communication by muscle movements can be considered as an ability to communicate the decision. The information will of course have to be presented in such a way as to enable the person to respond by simple 'yes' and 'no' answers.

ACTIVITY **3.2**

Assessing mental capacity

Reflect on a case where you had to assess whether a vulnerable adult had the mental capacity to make a specific decision. How did you go about undertaking this assessment? What was the nature of the decision that was needed? Why was this decision needed at this time and what would be the effect of making this decision one way or another? What was the impairment or disturbance in this case? How did you assess the person's ability to understand the information? What questions did you ask and why? What about the ability to retain the information? How did you assess the person's ability to use/weigh the information? Was the person able to communicate with you by any means? How did you document your assessment?

The Codes of Practice

The current Mental Health Act Code of Practice (Department of Health, 2015a) came into force in April 2015. It is a requirement of section 118 of the MHA 1983 that the Secretary of State prepares, and from time to time, revises a Code of Practice. The purpose of the Code is to give guidance to a range of professionals and these professionals must 'have regard' to the Code when they are applying the Act. The Code is considered to be statutory guidance and, whilst it does not have the force of statute, professionals must attach great weight to its guidance. The courts (*R (Munjaz) v Mersey Care NHS Trust* [2005] UKHL 58) have said that professionals must follow the Code of Practice unless they have cogent reasons not to, i.e. if a professional departs from the advice that is given in the Code of Practice then they need to have a very good reason for doing so and they need to clearly document their reasons. There are separate Codes for England and Wales.

The English Mental Health Act Code of Practice amounts to 464 pages and 40 chapters. Its guidance covers a wide range of subjects including:

- Guiding principles
- Mental disorder definition
- Human rights, equality and health inequalities
- The provision of information for patients, relatives and others
- The nearest relative
- Independent mental health advocates
- Attorneys and deputies
- Privacy, dignity and safety
- Wishes expressed in advance
- Confidentiality and information sharing
- Visiting patients in hospital
- The Tribunal
- Mental capacity and deprivation of liberty
- Applications for detention in hospital
- Emergency applications for detention
- Police powers and places of safety
- Transport of patients
- Holding powers
- Children and young people under the age of 18
- People with learning disabilities or autistic spectrum disorders
- People with personality disorders
- Patients concerned with criminal proceedings
- Appropriate medical treatment test
- Medical treatment
- Treatments subject to special rules and procedures
- Safe and therapeutic responses to behavioural disturbance
- Leave of absence
- Absence without leave
- Community treatment orders
- Guardianship
- Guardianship, leave of absence or CTO?

- Detention and CTO: renewal, extension and discharge

- Aftercare

- Care Programme Approach

- Receipt and scrutiny of documents

- Allocating and changing a responsible clinician

- The functions of hospital managers

- Hospital managers' discharge power

- Conflicts of interest

- Information for victims

The Mental Health Act Code of Practice is accompanied by the Mental Health Act Reference Guide (Department of Health, 2015b). The Reference Guide only covers England and is not considered to be statutory guidance. As a result it does not have the weight of the MHA Code of Practice. It is intended 'as a source of reference for people who want to understand the provisions of the Mental Health Act 1983'. It is a much longer document and explains in much more detail some of the more complex provisions of the MHA as amended by the 2007 Act. It is in parts much more easy to understand than the Act itself and it is a useful source of information and guidance for social workers and other professionals who wish to understand and apply the Act.

There are two more Codes of Practice that we need to consider here. Both of these relate to the Mental Capacity Act. They have the same weight as the MHA Code and form statutory guidance to which professionals must 'give regard'. There is the main MCA Code of Practice (Department for Constitutional Affairs, 2007), which was published in 2007, and then the supplement to the main MCA Code that covers the Deprivation of Liberty Safeguards (Ministry of Justice, 2008), which was published a year later. Both these documents are remarkable in terms of their accessibility and readability. Neither of them is particularly long and it is expected that every social worker working with adults should be familiar with their contents, especially the main MCA Code.

The main MCA Code of Practice stretches to 16 chapters and covers subjects such as:

- The statutory principles and how they should be applied

- How people should be helped to make their own decisions

- What is mental capacity and how it is assessed

- What the Act means when it talks about 'best interests'

- The protection offered by the Act for people providing care or treatment

- Lasting Powers of Attorney

- The role of the Court of Protection

- Advance decisions to refuse treatment

- Independent mental capacity advocates

- The relationship between the MCA and the MHA

The Deprivation of Liberty Safeguards (DOLS) Code of Practice is surprisingly easy to read given the often complex nature of the DOLS provisions it discusses. It is fairly short at only 125 pages and 11 chapters. It seeks to offer guidance and includes:

- What are the Deprivation of Liberty Safeguards and why were they introduced?

- What is a deprivation of liberty?

- How can a deprivation of liberty be applied for and authorised?

- The assessment process

- What happens when the assessment process is complete

- The role of the relevant person's representative

- Reviewing and ending an authorisation

- What happens if someone thinks that a person is being deprived of their liberty without authorisation

- The Court of Protection

These Codes of Practice, and the Reference Guide to the MHA, provide the social worker with a considerable amount of information and guidance on the application of mental health and mental capacity law. They are often more accessible and easier to understand than trying to read statute itself and as such they should be famil-iar documents to social workers and other professionals who work with vulnerable adults and those with mental health problems.

Key roles

Mental Health Act 1983

Approved mental health professional (AMHP)
An AMHP is a social worker, nurse, occupational therapist or psychologist who has untaken additional training approved by the Health and Care Professions Council (HCPC). The AMHP undertakes a range of roles under the MHA including: organis-ing assessments under the Act, making applications to a hospital for a person to be detained under the Act, conveying patients to hospital, applying to the magistrates' court for warrants to enter private premises to search for and remove people thought to be mentally disordered, considering applications for community treatment orders and making applications for patients to be received into guardianship.

Approved clinician (AC)
An approved clinician is usually a registered medical practitioner, but following the 2007 Act an approved clinician can now be a social worker, nurse, occupational

therapist or psychologist who has undertaken additional training to equip them for that role. The person in charge of a patient's treatment has to be an AC and that person is called the responsible clinician. ACs have a range of powers under the MHA.

Responsible clinician (RC)

The RC is the AC who is in charge of a patient's treatment in hospital under the Act. They have a range of duties and powers including: reviewing a patient's detention, granting leave of absence from hospital, deciding (with another professional) if a patient's detention should be renewed, discharging a patient from detention, blocking a nearest relative's order for a patient to be discharged, authorising a patient's medical treatment under the Act and deciding (with an AMHP's agreement) whether or not to discharge a patient under a community treatment order.

First Tier Tribunal (Mental Health) (MHT)

This is most commonly known as the Mental Health Tribunal and has the status of a court. However, unlike a court it sits in the hospital where the patient is detained and its role is to decide if the patient's detention should continue or the patient should be discharged from hospital. It has a range of other powers under the Act. It is made up of three people, the Tribunal Judge (who is legally qualified), the medical member (a consultant psychiatrist) and a specialist member (a person who has experience in mental disorder).

Hospital managers

Hospital managers are the people to whom applications to detain a patient are made and they are the people under whose authority patients are detained. They have a range of responsibilities and powers under the Act including: ensuring that patients and nearest relatives are provided with their rights and other information under the Act, transferring patients to another hospital, referring patients to the Mental Health Tribunal in certain cases and discharging patients from detention.

Second opinion approved doctor (SOAD)

The SOAD works for the Care Quality Commission (CQC) and has certain responsibilities with regard to authorising medical treatment under the Act, including medication and electroconvulsive therapy (ECT).

Independent mental health advocate (IMHA)

Each detained patient has a right of access to an IMHA. The role of the IMHA is to enable the patient to obtain information and understand: what section they are detained under and what restrictions apply to them, details of their medical treatment and why it is being given, and the authority under which the medical treatment is being given.

Nearest relative (NR)

The nearest relative is defined in the MHA and it is the AMHP who decides on the person who appears to be the patient's nearest relative. It is different from the 'next of kin' and a patient cannot chose who is his/her nearest relative. The nearest relative has a range of powers under the MHA, including: objecting to an application by an AMHP for their relative to be detained in hospital under section 3 or received under guardianship, making an application for their relative to be detained in hospital, requesting that the local social services authority consider their relative's case, discharging their relative from detention by applying to the hospital managers, applying to the Mental Health Tribunal for their relative to be discharged (in certain cases), and is to be consulted when the use of the Act is being considered.

Mental Capacity Act 2005 including the Deprivation of Liberty Safeguards

Best interests assessor (BIA)

The BIA is a social worker, nurse, occupational therapist or psychologist who has undertaken additional training to enable them to undertake this role. The BIA has specific roles under DOLS. They carry out the best interest assessment and can carry out several of the other required DOLS assessments as instructed by their local authority (the supervisory body).

Mental health assessor

The mental health assessor is also one of the DOLS assessors. They have to be a doctor with special experience in mental disorders and must have undertaken training to enable them to undertake this role. They carry out the mental health assessment, which is one of the six required assessments under DOLS. They can also carry out some of the other required assessments.

Decision maker

This is the person who has to make a specific decision on behalf of someone who lacks the capacity to make that decision for themself. The decision maker has to be sure that the person lacks the capacity to make the decision and then work out what would be in the best interests of the person. The decision maker can be different for different decisions that need to be made.

Lasting Power of Attorney (LPA)

The MCA provides for a person to make provision for a time when they lose the capacity to make decisions for themselves. One of the ways this can be done is for the person to appoint someone to make decisions for them when they lose capacity. This is called making an LPA. There are two types of LPA: property and affairs (including financial matters), and personal welfare (including healthcare and consent to medical treatment).

Deputy

If a person loses capacity to make specific decisions before making an LPA then an application can be made to the Court of Protection for a deputy to be appointed. This deputy can make decisions regarding property and affairs. More rarely will the court appoint a deputy for personal welfare and then only in the most difficult of cases.

Court of Protection (COP)

This court was set up by the MCA to deal with decision making for adults who may lack the capacity to make specific decisions for themselves. The court, as well as dealing with financial matters, deals with serious decisions affecting healthcare and personal welfare matters. This court has the same powers and authority as the High Court and is able to set legal precedent. This court also considers appeals regarding the DOLS provisions.

Relevant person's representative (RPR)

A RPR is appointed once a supervisory body issues an authorisation for a person to be deprived of their liberty under DOLS. This is normally a close relative who is able to keep in contact with the relevant person (the person who is the subject of the DOLS authorisation) and has certain rights under the DOLS provisions, including requesting an IMCA, making complaints, and making applications to the Court of Protection on behalf of the relevant person.

Independent mental capacity advocate (IMCA)

IMCAs have a role to help particularly vulnerable people who lack the capacity to make important decisions and who have no family or friends that it would be suitable to consult. These important decisions relate to serious medical treatment or change of accommodation. IMCAs also have a role under DOLS, as both the relevant person and the relevant person's representative have a statutory right of access to an IMCA.

Supervisory body (SB)

This is the local authority within which the care home or hospital is located. The SB has to consider applications from managing authorities for a standard authorisation under the DOLS provisions. The SB is responsible for organising the BIA and mental health assessors to carry out the six required assessments and then issuing the managing authority with the standard authorisation if the six requirements are met.

Managing authority (MA)

This is the registered manager of the care home or independent hospital, or in the case of an NHS hospital the trust responsible for the running of the hospital. The MA has the responsibility of applying to the SB for a standard authorisation if they think they may have anyone under their care who is being deprived of their liberty.

CHAPTER SUMMARY

- The purpose of the Mental Health Act is to do with the treatment of people who have a mental disorder and provides for the state to deprive them of or restrict their liberty in certain circumstances.

- Mental disorder is defined in section 1 of the Act as 'any disorder or disability of mind'.

- The Mental Capacity Act is mainly concerned with people who lack the capacity to make specific decisions for themselves.

- Mental incapacity is defined in section 2 of the Act as a person being unable to make a decision for himself in relation to the matter because of an impairment or a disturbance in the functioning of the mind or brain.

(Continued)

CHAPTER SUMMARY *Continued*

- The mental incapacity test is made up of two parts: the diagnostic test (set out above) and the functional test. The latter involves assessing whether or not the person can: understand the information in relation to the decision; retain the information; use or weigh the information and then communicate the decision.

- Both Acts have their associated Codes of Practice which social workers must follow unless they have 'cogent' reasons not to.

- There are a number of key professional roles and bodies within the two Acts and social workers need to understand these.

FURTHER READING

Brown, R (2009) *The Approved Mental Health Professional's Guide to Mental Health Law*, 2nd edition. Exeter: Learning Matters.
This book is a good starting point if you want to read further into the Mental Health Act 1983.

Department of Constitutional Affairs (2007) *Mental Capacity Act 2005 Code of Practice*. London.
This Code of Practice is very accessible and readable and should be read by every social worker who works with vulnerable adults.

Part II
Application to practice

Chapter 4
Principles and values

Introduction

Both the Mental Health Act 1983 and the Mental Capacity Act 2005 are underpinned by principles which govern how these Acts should be applied by professionals to people who come within the Acts' provisions. It is important that social workers working with people with a mental disorder or those who lack the capacity to make a specific decision are able to understand and apply these principles in their work. You do not have to delve very far into experiences of mental health service users to find some very negative and distressing accounts of forced medication and incarceration, such as in Read and Reynolds (1996). It is tempting to think that such negative experiences of mental health services are something of the past. Unfortunately not. The Care Quality Commission (CQC) in a report on monitoring the Mental Health Act (CQC, 2014) states that it continues to see blanket rules and restrictive practices being imposed on all patients in three quarters of wards visited because of 'hospital policy' regardless of the needs of and risk imposed by individual patients. The CQC also continues to see a lack of evidence of patients involved in drawing up their care plans in 27 per cent of cases (CQC, 2014: p3). The principles discussed in this chapter should ensure that when patients have to be treated against their will, or decisions are made for them because they are not able to, such practices do not continue.

Decision making in social work is not always clear-cut: sometimes you are asked to reconcile several seemingly conflicting values. This is especially apparent when a vulnerable person is making decisions or acting in a way that is causing them, and/or other people, harm. Do you intervene to prevent the harm knowing that it will have a negative impact on their independence? As a social worker you have a duty to maintain the safety of service users. How do you manage these sometimes competing requirements? When making decisions regarding people with a mental disorder or those who lack capacity to make decisions, it is important that you apply these principles to your decision making. As we will see applying these principles are consistent with your social work value base and will help you resolve ethical dilemmas as to how you should act in a given situation.

In this chapter we will consider each set of principles in turn, thinking about how they impact on practice. We will then discuss how these principles relate to social work professional standards and values. We will then go on to explore a key dilemma in this area of social work: the conflict between promoting independence and autonomy of personal decision making on one hand, and preventing vulnerable people coming to harm, or harming others, on the other.

Mental Health Act guiding principles

The Mental Health Act guiding principles are to be found in Chapter 1 of the MHA Code of Practice for England (Department of Health, 2015a). There are similar principles in the Code of Practice for Wales (Welsh Assembly Government, 2008). The English Code has five guiding principles whilst the Welsh Code has 29 principles organised under four headings: empowerment, equity, effectiveness and efficiency. We will focus on the English principles and social workers in Wales should familiarise themselves with the Welsh principles. As can been seen from the headings there are many similarities between the two sets of principles. These principles are not statutory as they are not to be found in legislation but, as we discussed in the last chapter, professionals have a legal duty to have regard to the Code of Practice and if they depart from the Code they need to have cogent reasons for doing so. So, whilst these guiding principles do not have the full force of law, you are required to have regard to them in your decision making. If you do not, you will have to explain why you did not apply them.

Least restriction option and maximising independence (paras 1.2–1.6)

This principle talks about minimising restrictions on people who come within the Act's provisions. It states that if it is possible to provide treatment without detaining the patient, then the patient should not be detained. Services should be available for patients to prevent mental health crises and reduce the use of detention. If a person is going to be detained then it must be for the shortest time possible and delivered as close as possible to where the patient would like to be.

> Any restrictions should be the minimum necessary to safely provide the care or treatment required having regard to whether the purpose for the restriction can be achieved in a way that is less restrictive of the person's rights and freedom of action.

> (para 1.5)

This is a simple principle to understand but can be overlooked in practice. This principle re-enforces the need to only use the powers within the Act if it is strictly necessary, and if so, for the shortest possible time. This will sometimes involve trying to avoid the need for detention by using services in the community such as home treatment or crisis services. It can also mean trying to use informal admission to hospital (admitting a patient to hospital but not detaining them under the Act). If you are working with a person who is experiencing mental distress, using the Act to detain them in hospital should be a last resort and can only be considered when other less restrictive options have failed or the risks are too great to be managed in the community. Also, hospitals should avoid the use of blanket rules or restrictions that apply to all patients regardless of need or risk.

Even when a patient is detained in hospital for treatment and you think about all the restrictions being imposed on them just by being in a psychiatric hospital, as well as the ones imposed as part of their treatment and risk management plans, how do you know that in-patient staff have considered this principle in devising these plans? As a social worker working with a person who is currently detained in hospital, you can discuss these issues with the multi-disciplinary team to enable them to think about the need to minimise the restrictions on the patient whilst preventing harm. This principle supports you in asking questions of the multi-disciplinary team as to the reasons for the restrictions and exploring with them, and the patient, care plans that minimise restrictions. The Care Quality Commission (CQC) found that in 10 per cent of cases there is no evidence that the least restriction principle has been considered in care plans (CQC, 2014: p27).

Empowerment and involvement (paras 1.7–1.12)

This talks about how patients should be involved in decisions about their care and treatment.

> Patients should be given the opportunity to be involved in planning, developing and reviewing their own care and treatment to help ensure that it is delivered in a way that is as appropriate and effective for them as possible. Wherever possible, care plans should be produced in consultation with the patient.

> (para 1.7)

This principle states that the patient's choices and views should be fully recorded and when the clinical team makes decisions which are contrary to the patient's views the reasons for this should be explained to the patient and fully documented. This principle also talks about the involvement of carers and advocates if the patient wishes.

We talk about how social workers can apply this principle when working with patients in Chapter 6.

Respect and dignity (paras 1.13 and 1.14)

Social workers spend a considerable amount of time during their training, and after qualifying, working with diversity issues. As a result social workers are often more comfortable and skilled at addressing these issues than their health colleagues.

> People taking decisions under the Act must recognise and respect the diverse needs, values and circumstances of each patient, including their race, religion, culture, gender, age, sexual orientation and any disability. They must consider the patient's views, wishes and feelings (whether expressed at the time or in advance), so far as they are reasonably ascertainable, and follow those wishes wherever practicable and consistent with the purpose of the decision. There must be no unlawful discrimination.
>
> (para 1.4)

When working with patients who find themselves under the provisions of the MHA, you need to consider the diverse range of their needs and make sure that the other professionals working with the patient understand those needs and consider them when making decisions. However, this principle also talks about considering the views, wishes and feelings of the patient and following them where possible. This means that in-patient staff have to take time to speak to each patient to understand their views as well as making sure that they have gathered enough information in order to meet the full range of their diverse needs.

ACTIVITY **4 . 1**

Provision of information on hospital wards

Think about a recent occasion you have had to go onto a hospital ward, either in a professional capacity or a personal one. What information was available either on posters, in leaflets or provided for you that gave you confidence that the ward staff understood or at least had some awareness of your specific needs as a woman, a Black man, an Asian woman, a gay man or lesbian, a person who uses a wheelchair, a person with learning disabilities, etc.? Was the information understandable and accessible? What information would you have liked that was not available and how could this have been provided?

Purpose and effectiveness (paras 1.15–1.17)

This principle sets out the purpose of providing treatment under the Act and that such treatment should be effective and safe.

> Patients should be offered treatment and care in environments that are safe for them, staff and any visitors and are supportive and therapeutic. Practitioners should deliver a range of treatments which focus on positive clinical and personal outcomes, where appropriate. Care plans for detained patients should focus on maximising recovery and ending detention as soon as possible.
>
> (para 1.6)

This is the need to make sure, if a patient is detained in hospital (or subject to community powers), that resources are made available to enable the patient's needs are met, and they are not kept in hospital longer than necessary. This principle guards against detaining patients in hospital without providing any effective treatment or care.

Efficiency and equity (paras 1.18–1.21)

This principle states that mental health needs should be given equal priority to physical health conditions.

> Where patients are subject to compulsory detention, health and social care agencies should work together to deliver a programme of care that, as far as practicable, minimises the duration of detention, facilitates safe discharge from hospital and takes into account the patient's wishes.
>
> (para 1.19)

This principle focuses on agencies needing to work together to provide effective care that minimises delays.

ACTIVITY 4.2

Applying Mental Health Act principles

Think about a person you are working with in the community who has some sort of mental disorder that means they need social care or health services. When it came to involving the person in decisions about their care, how were these principles applied? What went well and what could have been done better?

Mental Capacity Act principles

The Mental Capacity Act principles are to be found in section 1 of the Act and as such they are statutory principles. You have to do more than have 'regard' to them, as applying these principles are a statutory requirement and if you do not you could be acting unlawfully. As the Act applies to England and Wales, the principles are the same for both countries. Chapter 2 of the MCA Code of Practice (Department of Constitutional Affairs, 2007) gives guidance on how these statutory principles should be applied and scenarios to illustrate how the principles work in practice. The introduction to Chapter 2 of the MCA Code states:

> Section 1 of the Act sets out the five 'statutory principles' – the values that underpin the legal requirements in the Act. The Act is intended to be enabling and supportive of people who lack capacity, not restricting or controlling of their lives. It aims to protect people who lack capacity to make particular decisions, but also to maximise their ability to make decisions, or to participate in decision-making, as far as they are able to do so.

A person must be assumed to have capacity unless it is established that they lack capacity

This principle sets out the statutory presumption that everyone is assumed to have capacity to make his or her own decisions. If they do not have the capacity to make a specific decision then it is up to the professional reaching that decision to prove that the person does not have the capacity. It is not up to the person to prove they do have the capacity to make the decision in question. In other words, the starting assumption must always be that an individual has the capacity, until there is proof that they do not (MCA Code, para 2.4).

A person is not to be treated as unable to make a decision unless all practicable steps to help him to do so have been taken without success

Before deciding that a person does not have the capacity to make a decision, all practicable steps must be taken to help that person make the decision. Such steps include: using different forms of communication, providing information in a more accessible form, treating a medical condition that might be affecting their capacity, or having a structured programme to improve a person's decision-making skills (MCA Code, para 2.7). If the decision or action required is not urgent, then time should be taken to support the person to make the decision for themselves. It may be that the person is more alert and responsive in a particular part of the day so that is the time that efforts can be made to enable the person to make a decision.

A person is not to be treated as unable to make a decision merely because he makes an unwise decision

A person with capacity is allowed to make a decision that others think is unwise. Just because a person appears to be making an unwise decision, it should not be automatically assumed that they lack the capacity to make that decision. Social workers do need to be mindful that their duties to safeguard vulnerable adults do not cause them to override the right of these adults to make decisions that could be considered to be unwise (if the vulnerable adult has the capacity to make these decisions). When assessing whether or not a person lacks the capacity to make a decision, it is very important that you assess the quality of their decision making (i.e. the process they go through in order to arrive at their decision), not the quality of their decision (i.e. the outcome of the process of making the decision). It may be felt that a person lacks capacity because they are not accepting that they need social care services, for example. There are plenty of people who do not accept they need help and support; this does not automatically mean that they lack capacity.

This does not mean that a person making unwise decisions should not be assessed to see if they have capacity, especially if such decisions are putting them at risk of harm, or are obviously out of character. However, account does need to be taken of their past decisions and choices and any changes that have taken place recently, before coming to the conclusion that the current decisions indicate that the person does not have the capacity to make them.

An act done, or decision made, under this Act for or on behalf of a person who lacks capacity must be done, or made, in his best interests

If a person lacks capacity to make a particular decision, then those charged with making that decision on the person's behalf, needs to make that decision in the person's best interests. This is different from making the decision that the person would have made had they had capacity. The MCA Code (para 2.13) states that it is impossible to give a single description of what 'best interests' are because they depend on the individual and the specific circumstances they face at the time. Section 4 of the Act sets out a checklist of the steps you need to follow in reaching a best interests decision and we discuss this in detail in Chapter 6.

Before the act is done, or the decision is made, regard must be given to whether the purpose for which it is needed can be as effectively achieved in a way that is less restrictive of the person's rights and freedom of action

This is similar to the least restrictive principle in the MHA Code. However, there is an important difference: the MHA principle talks about the *least* restrictive option, and the MCA talks about the need to act in a way that is *less* restrictive. Therefore, under the MHA if you have a range of options you must go for the least restrictive one available, and under the MCA if you have a less restrictive option you must use it but you do not have to use the least restrictive option. This gives you more flexibility in your decision making whilst making sure the person is safe from harm. The MCA Code states (para 2.15), 'Where there is more than one option, it is important to explore ways that would be less restrictive or allow the most freedom for a person who lacks capacity to make the decision in question'. If the less restrictive option is not in the person's best interests then it cannot be used.

ACTIVITY *4.3*

Applying Mental Capacity Act principles

Think about a person you have worked with who, at least some of the time, has lacked the capacity to make decisions about their care. How were these principles applied in this case? What steps did you take to help the person make the decision? How did you make sure that you were not making a judgement about the person's ability to make the decision based on your view that the decision was unwise? How did you ensure that the decision made on behalf of the person was in their best interests? Could you have made a different decision that would have been a less restrictive option?

Social work professional standards

Embedded in the nature of social work is this tension between care and control. Social workers are required to be enabling and empowering to those with whom they work, while at the same time preventing harm.

The Health and Care Professions Council (HCPC) standards of proficiency (SoP) for social workers in England set out what is expected of you as a social worker. Standard 2.2 talks about the need to promote the best interests of service users and carers at all times and standard 2.7 sets out the need to respect and uphold the rights, dignity, values and autonomy of every service user and carer. Welsh social care standard 1 (Care Council for Wales, undated) talks about protecting the rights and promoting the interests of service users and carers. How can you as a social worker promote rights and best interests when the person you are working with is being deprived of their liberty and having rights taken away? As we have seen in Chapter 2, people's experiences of mental health services have not always been positive. Mental health services, and especially hospitals, have been seen as oppressive and disabling. When visiting people on mental health wards or in care homes, you may find things or see things that make you feel uncomfortable. This can be a drive to ask questions, to critically explore what is going on (Rutter and Brown, 2012: p29). Your social work values and these principles should help inform you as to how things should be.

However, promoting rights and independence of service users and protecting them from harm, or from harming others, are not necessarily mutually exclusive. The Welsh standards 3 and 4 see these things as two sides of the same coin: they talk about promoting independence whilst protecting them from harm, and respecting rights whilst seeking to ensure that the service user's behaviour does not harm themself or others. The HCPC standard 2.3 talks about safeguarding vulnerable adults, while standard 2.4 sets out the need to address practices that present a risk to or from service users.

Making decisions about how to safeguard vulnerable people from harm can raise difficult ethical issues, as there is a need for responses to risk of harm to be proportionate to that harm. People can come to harm within hospitals or care homes as well as losing independence and their ability to live independently.

Making difficult decisions

Consider a case where there is no clear best interest decision, and all the available options appear to be equally difficult. What would inform your decision making when considering options that are all potentially harmful in some way or another? What factors would you take into account? How do your social work values help to inform your decision making?

Tension between care and control

Brown (2009: p2) discusses these issues in relation to the tension between civil liberties versus welfarism. For him these tensions are based on differing understandings of mental disorder. A civil libertarian approach, if it accepted the existence of mental disorder at all, would adopt the view that people should make their own decisions about their treatment for a mental disorder as with a physical disorder. They would argue that there does not need to be laws relating to mental disorder at all. However, they might consider law relating to mental incapacity in specific limited circumstances.

A welfarist approach would see that it is necessary to intervene against someone's will to protect a person from themselves or to protect others from them. Such an approach would argue for more resources and use of more restrictive options to protect people from harm. It would consider the views and wishes of the person to be secondary to the need to protect them, and others, from harm.

ACTIVITY **4.5**

Welfarism or civil liberties

If you placed welfarism and civil liberties approaches on opposite ends of a continuum, where would you place yourself? What about medical professionals? People who have had experiences of being detained under the MHA? Carers for people with mental health problems?

For Bogg (2010) this tension (between welfarism and civil liberties) is best articulated as between enforcement and empowerment. For her empowerment is defined as:

The process by which the individual can make choices, express their own views and preferences, influence their own situations and take control and responsibility for their own actions.

(Bogg, 2010: p51)

For Bogg (2010: p56), enforcement is about the application of power by the professional, and while this dynamic is most clearly seen in the roles of the approved mental health professional and the best interests assessor, all mental health professionals are influenced by the power differential between the professional and the person who uses mental health services. Therefore, enforcement, if it is applied, needs to operate within a value base and ethical framework.

> With regard to the role of ethics, the professional needs to ensure that their actions are undertaken in an appropriate, proportionate and informed manner. The ability to exercise coercion should never be downplayed: the aim of a transparent application of power requires the worker to identify the power dynamics and to ensure that the individual's rights are observed at all times. Coercion is neither a threat nor an incentive: it should only be used if it becomes necessary according to the criteria set down in law and disagreement between worker and user is never sufficient justification.

(Bogg, 2010: 57)

It could be argued that people who are detained under the Mental Health Act need not be totally disempowered. As we will discuss in Chapter 6, patients' views need to be obtained, considered and carried out (unless there are good reasons not to do so) even if they are detained. Roberts et al. (2008) discuss the role of choice in the care of the detained patient. They argue that detention is sometimes necessary as it would be 'unkind or downright negligent to support perverse or morbid choices that may be at significant variance with a person's values when well'. They go on to discuss that patients should be given choices with regard to their care but these need to be real and available choices. However, they argue that patients should not be able to make choices that would be detrimental to their recovery and discharge from hospital: 'Activity itself should not be optional, but which activity Stephen decides to pursue can be – a range of activities should be available that tune into his values and interests' (Roberts et al., 2008: p175).

These dual roles of empowerment and enforcement can be difficult for you to manage, and as Bogg (2010: p57) argues, this is something that professionals are required to reconcile within themselves. Using reflective and critical examination of your practice will ensure that the power relationship is acknowledged, and that your practice is at all times ethical.

CASE STUDY

Michael

Michael is a young man with mild to moderate learning disabilities. He lives in a room in a shared house. He has a supportive family who live in the neighbouring town. He does not work and he is in receipt of benefits. Recently the police have become concerned about his behaviour and his vulnerability. Two young women have complained that Michael has made unwelcome sexual advances to them. The police do not think that sexual offences have been committed but are concerned that they may in the future. Michael told the police that other residents are coming into his room and taking his money. They ask him for money for cigarettes and drugs and he hands it over. He says that he is happy to do this because they are his friends. His mother reports that he often does not have enough money left to pay for food. An adult safeguarding referral has been made to the local authority and you have been allocated the case.

Apply the ethical approaches we have discussed in this chapter to this case. How do they inform how you respond? How would you seek to address the issues raised by Michael's behaviour? How do you manage the tension between empowerment and enforcement?

CHAPTER SUMMARY

- The Mental Health Act guiding principles are found in the MHA Code of Practice.

- The Mental Capacity Act guiding principles are found within the Act itself in section 1.

- Both these sets of principles are consistent with social work professional standards.

- There are times when you may experience a tension between your duty to promote independence and empower the people with whom you are working, and your duty to keep people safe and use enforcement powers. Reflective and critical examination of your practice should enable you to practise ethically at all times.

FURTHER READING

Bogg, D (2010) *Values and Ethics in Mental Health Practice*. Exeter: Learning Matters.

This book will help you think about your social work values and how to put them into practice in working with people who experience mental distress.

Department of Health (2015) *Mental Health Act 1983: Code of Practice*. London: TSO.

Chapter 1 sets out the guiding principles which should be considered when making decisions in relation to care and treatment provided under the Mental Health Act 1983.

Chapter 5

Assessment

Introduction

In this chapter we are going to examine how people get assessed under the Mental Health Act 1983 (MHA) and contrast this with the provisions of the Mental Capacity Act 2005 (MCA). As a social worker, you will need to know when you need to make a referral for an assessment under the MHA, and what happens when you make that referral. We will consider what information the approved mental health professional (AMHP) will want from you when you make a referral and how the assessment is set up and carried out. The possible outcomes from an assessment will be examined by considering the sections under which a patient can be detained in hospital. The role of the AMHP in conveying the patient from the place of assessment to the hospital in which they are going to be detained will be explored, as well as some of the practical considerations that need to be made when admitting a patient to hospital. We will briefly consider some police powers under the MHA including the use of a warrant to remove a patient from private premises and the power to take a person to a place of safety for assessment.

As a social worker who is not an AMHP, you may feel anxious or unsure about either when to make a referral for an assessment under the MHA or what to do when you have made such a referral. You may wonder if you have any role during the assessment process and if so what this is. If you are working with a person who is compulsorily admitted to hospital, you should expect to be involved in the whole process. You should avoid thinking that once you have made the referral, you no longer have a role to play. This chapter will help you to understand the process of assessing a person under the Act, the decision-making process, and how the person gets to hospital if that is the outcome of the assessment. It will also help you in your discussions with the AMHP about what part, if any, you should play as the assessment and any resultant admission unfolds.

Assessments under the MCA can be undertaken by a broader range of people including non-professionals, so we will consider who can assess a person's capacity to make a specific decision and in what circumstances.

Mental Health Act assessments

Requesting an assessment

Having considered the guiding principles of the Mental Health Act in the last chapter, we know that a decision to detain a patient in hospital is one taken as a last resort. We also know from Chapter 3 that the purpose of the Mental Health Act is to meet the needs of people with a mental disorder primarily by arranging for their admission to hospital. As a result, before you consider making a referral for an assessment under the MHA, you need to have considered:

- What is the evidence that the person has a mental disorder?

- Is there a least restrictive alternative to admission to hospital such as support from a crisis or home treatment team?

- If the person needs to be admitted to hospital can they be admitted without using the Act, i.e. can they be admitted informally?

Once you have decided that you need to make a referral for an assessment under the Act, you have considered least restrictive options, and possibly talked to any medical practitioners or mental health professionals who know the patient, what next? Before you contact the AMHP service, you need to gather the information that the AMHP will require in order to set up the MHA assessment. Do not presume that they will already know this information, even in the case of a patient who has been detained under the Act on many occasions. Information changes and it is your role as the referrer to provide the AMHP service with the most up-to-date information. The information the AMHP will need includes:

- The full name of the patient and the name by which they prefer to be known.

- The patient's date of birth.

- The patient's ethnicity, gender identity and living situation.

- Their address.

- Where the patient is to be found if they are not or will not be at their home address for the assessment.

- Who are the relatives of the patient and their contact details. This is to enable the AMHP to determine who is their nearest relative and as such you should give them the details of anyone who they live with (including how long for if possible), details of their spouse (married including same sex marriage and civil partners as well as living together as spouse for six months or more), details of children and if they are 18 or over. If there are no such relatives then you will need to provide details of parents, brothers or sisters, grandparents, uncles or aunts (blood relatives only) and nephews or nieces. Also you will need to tell the AMHP if any of these relatives provide care for the patient. You may not have some of this information but find out as much as you can.

- The details of the patient's general practitioner.

- Why you are requesting an assessment and what alternatives have been tried.

- Names and contact details of professionals involved with the patient.

- Brief social history of the patient including their current circumstances.

- Brief health history including previous treatment for mental disorder and previous periods of detention in hospital.

- The risks to the patient and risks from the patient.

- Any specific needs that the patient may have due to a disability, cultural background or language.

You may not have all this information to hand and the situation may be quite urgent so you may not have time to gather all this information. However, the more information you are able to quickly pass on to the AMHP service, the more likely you will get the response that is most appropriate for the patient.

Duty to assess

Section 13(1) of the Act sets out that if a local social services authority (a local authority) has reason to believe that a patient 'within their area' needs to be admitted to hospital under the Act, they must arrange for an AMHP to consider the patient's case. The patient only needs to be 'within their area' and does not need to live or reside within the area of the local authority. It is often interpreted by AMHPs as a 'where the body is' rule. It is the duty of the AMHP from the local authority area where the patient is to be currently found to 'consider the patient's case'. Sometimes it may be better for an AMHP from another area to consider the case, especially if they are from the area where the patient lives and services in that area know the patient. However, whilst another AMHP service may agree to assess the patient, the legal duty rests on the AMHP service where the patient is currently located. Local authorities often have protocols in place to cover such situations especially if the patient appears in a neighbouring local authority area from the one where they live. However, the AMHP service where the patient currently finds themself is responsible for taking the referral and making the arrangements for an AMHP to assess the patient. As there is sometimes debate as to which local authority should carry out the assessment, always make the referral to the local authority where the patient is currently located. Respectfully point out that it is the local authority 'where the body is' that has a duty to make the arrangements to 'consider the case' and ask them to resolve the situation with another local authority if there is a difference of opinion.

If you are making a referral for a patient who is already in hospital or police station, there may be local protocols that cover which AMHP service should assess them. For example, one hospital (general or psychiatric) may take patients from several local authority areas, and it would not be possible for the local authority in which the hospital is based to carry out all the assessments. In such circumstances it is usually the local authority where the patient lives that would carry out the assessments. If you are likely to be making referrals for assessments under the Act regularly as part of your work, it would be a good idea to make sure you are familiar with local protocols so that you know what to do when the time comes.

Setting up the assessment

Once the AMHP service has accepted the referral, the case will be allocated to an AMHP and they will proceed to set up the assessment. How quickly the assessment takes place will depend on the risks and needs of the patient and other demands on the AMHP service. If you think that the referral is particularly urgent, you need to have the evidence to support your opinion. You also need to consider whether you can make yourself available to support the patient during the assessment and any resultant admission to hospital. This is particularly important if you know the patient well and it is likely that the patient is going to be assessed by an AMHP and doctors who they have not met before. It is a good idea to discuss with the AMHP what role you should take in the assessment, if any. It can be helpful for the person being assessed to have a familiar face present, and if you know any relatives you could have an important role to support them through what can be a very distressing process. It is the role of the AMHP to decide who should be present at an assessment and it can get very crowded, especially if other professionals and/or the police need to attend.

Most assessments under the Act require an AMHP and two registered medical practitioners (medical doctors). One has to have special experience of working with mental disorder (called a section 12 approved doctor) and it is preferable that one doctor has previous knowledge of the patient. If neither doctor knows the patient, the AMHP will usually arrange for two section 12 doctors to attend. While it is the duty of the doctors to find the bed to which the patient is going to be admitted (if that is the outcome of the assessment), it is usually the AMHP who checks that there is a bed available. Not having a bed should not delay the assessment, because the AMHP will not know if they need to admit the person until they carry out the assessment with the two doctors. However, the AMHP cannot make an application to detain the patient until they have a bed and the hospital has agreed to take the patient.

Once the AMHP has arranged for two doctors to attend, they need to think about when and where the assessment is going to take place. If the person lives alone then the AMHP has to be pretty certain that they are going to be at home when the assessing team arrives. This gives rise to a difficult decision that the AHMP has to make: do they let the person know that they are coming? Usually an assessment under the Act is not arranged until other alternatives have been considered. There is therefore a chance that a person will avoid being assessed under the Act if they know it is going to take place. However, it is rarely pleasant for the person to have at least three (usually more) people turn up at their home unexpectedly. If you know the person being assessed, you may be able to support the AMHP and the person to make sure the assessment takes place in the best circumstances possible. If there are relatives living with the person then it is very likely that they will be involved in the arrangements. You need to be aware that this may put relatives in a difficult position because they may be asked to withhold information from the patient until the assessment, and this may have a detrimental impact on their relationship with the patient following the assessment. If you know the person and their family, you may be asked for your views on these issues.

The AMHP will then think about who else needs to be present at the assessment. They may ask you (if you are already working with the patient) to attend for the reasons we have already discussed. They may ask for other professionals to be present, especially if they need specialist advice. There may be a need for an interpreter. They may ask for the police to attend, especially if there is a risk to others present at the assessment or there is a risk that the patient may abscond. We will consider the role of the police in more detail later in the chapter.

Interviewing the patient

An AMHP can only make an application for detention once they have interviewed the patient 'in a suitable manner' (MHA, s13(2)). The Act does not define what 'suitable manner' means but it does involve a discussion with the patient where they are able to express their views. It may mean that the patient would like someone present to support them in expressing their views (MHA Code, para 14.53) and they should be offered the opportunity to speak to the AMHP alone (unless there is a risk of physical harm to the AMHP) (MHA Code, para 14.54). The doctors also need to carry out a medical examination of the patient (MHA Code, para 14.71). Before the interview starts the AMHP needs to introduce themself and the other professionals present as well as explain the purpose of the assessment and the roles of the professionals present (MHA Code, para 14.51). If you are aware of any particular views or wishes that the patient has regarding admission or treatment in hospital, you need to make sure the AMHP aware is of them so that they discuss them with the patient.

In reaching their decision the AMHP also needs to consider the views of relatives, and especially the views of the nearest relative (the person appearing to be the nearest relative is defined in section 26 of the Act and will be examined in Chapter 10). You may want to think about how you will need to support relatives in expressing their views. Some relatives may be so upset or distressed that they find it difficult to express their views, or on the other hand, they may feel that professionals know best and that their views are not important. Whatever the situation it is important that the AMHP is able to consider the views of relatives as part of the assessment process.

Making the decision

Once the interview has taken place the two doctors will have to decide whether or not to recommend that the patient be admitted to hospital. It is best practice that the doctors carry out their examination at the same time and with the AMHP but this is not always possible. The doctors can carry out their examinations of the patient separately but no more than seven days apart. Their role is to provide medical expertise and decide if the patient is mentally disordered within the meaning of the Act. As we have already considered, if the patient is not mentally disordered then the Mental Health Act does not apply to them. Once they have decided that the patient is mentally disordered, they have to decide if it is of a nature *or* degree to warrant admission to hospital. The MHA Code states that 'nature' refers to the particular mental disorder from which the patient is suffering, while 'degree' refers to the current manifestation of the disorder (para 14.6). The doctors also need to consider the risk to the patient's health, *or* their safety, *or* the need to protect others from the patient. They also need to consider if the patient can be admitted to hospital informally (MHA, s131). If they consider the patient needs to be detained in hospital they make their recommendations to the AMHP on the statutory form(s).

Before making their decision the AMHP has to be satisfied that the statutory criteria for detention are met, and that in all the circumstances of the case detention in hospital is the most appropriate way of providing the care and medical treatment the patient needs (MHA, s13(2)). As you can see, the AMHP has a wide discretion in reaching their decision. Just because the doctors have recommended that the patient be detained in hospital, it does not mean that the AMHP has to agree with them. The AMHP will take into account the wishes and views of the patient, their relatives and other professionals involved with the patient before coming to their decision. You may be asked for your opinion, whether you are present at the assessment or not, so be prepared to give your views if asked. The AMHP has to exercise their own judgement to come to an independent decision and the local authority cannot tell them what their decision should be (MHA Code, para 14.52). If the AMHP decides the patient needs to be detained, they then make an application to the hospital, which has agreed to accept the patient, on the statutory form. Once that form is completed and signed the patient is in the lawful custody of the AMHP and the AMHP has all the powers of a police constable over the patient

(MHA, s137(2)). The AMHP then needs to make the arrangements for the patient to be conveyed to hospital.

The AMHP does not have to make their decision straight away. They may want to assess the patient's response to alternatives to admission such as home treatment and/or medication. The AMHP has 14 days from the date of the second medical recommendation to make their application (for sections 2 and 3). If you are aware that the AMHP is using these 14 days as part of their ongoing assessment of the patient, you may need to keep in regular contact with the patient and keep the AMHP informed of events.

Informal admission

One of the outcomes of an assessment is that the patient can be admitted to hospital informally. This can be on the basis of their consent or if they lack capacity to make that decision using the provisions of the MCA.

Section 131 of the Act states that there is nothing in the Act that prevents a patient being admitted to, or remaining in hospital, without any application being made, i.e. a patient can been admitted without needing to be detained. We have discussed valid consent in Chapter 2, and in order for a patient to be able to give valid consent they need to have sufficient knowledge of the purpose, nature, likely effects and risks of that treatment, including the likelihood of its success and any alternatives to it (MHA Code, para 24.34). Therefore, in order for a patient to give consent to admission and treatment in hospital following an MHA assessment, the assessing team need to ensure that the patient has sufficient information about what is proposed and what admission to hospital entails in order to make their decision. Such information would include:

- Details of ward rules, such as prohibited items, visiting times, activities, etc.
- That they may be prescribed medication and what could happen if they refuse medication.
- Details of the treatment they would be offered and why.
- Details of observations to which they could be subject.
- That they might be prevented from leaving if the staff feel that it is not safe; or that they might need to only go out with an escort; and what would happen if they insisted on going out against advice.
- That they may be prevented from discharging themselves if the clinical team do not think it is safe including the holding powers under MHA section 5.
- They might be searched.
- They might be restrained if they present a risk to themselves or others.

Informal admission should not be offered under threat of detention if the patient does not agree as 'permission given under any unfair or undue pressure is not consent' (MHA Code, para 24.34). If you are involved in a discussion with the patient around informal admission, you may be asked your views as to whether or not the patient is able to understand this information and use it to give valid consent to informal admission.

If the patient lacks the capacity to consent to admission and treatment in hospital, then the MCA could be considered as the least restrictive option. This would involve a decision that the person lacks capacity under sections 2 and 3 of the MCA followed by a decision that it would be in the patient's best interests (MCA, s5). These decisions would need to be documented, giving clear reasons for finding that the patient lacks the capacity to make the decision and why admission to hospital is in their best interests. (See Chapter 6 for a discussion about making a best interests decision.) If the patient will be deprived of their liberty by being cared for in hospital, section 5 of the MCA cannot be used (MHA Code, para 13.35) and the MHA or the Deprivation of Liberty Safeguards (DOLS) will need to be considered. (See Chapter 9 for more information on DOLS.)

Admission for assessment

A patient can be detained in hospital in order to have an assessment of their mental disorder. The legal criteria (also called legal grounds) are set out in section 2 of the MHA. This section provides for a patient to be admitted to hospital for up to 28 days. This section cannot be renewed so at the end of the 28 days, the patient has to be either discharged; able to stay in hospital informally; or further detained but under a different section of the Act (section 3). The grounds for section 2 include that the patient has a mental disorder of a nature *or* degree which warrants the detention of the patient for an assessment (or assessment followed by treatment) and that the patient 'ought' to be detained for their health *or* their safety *or* the protection of others. It is a myth that the patient has to be at risk of harm to either themselves or others before they can be detained. They can be detained just on the grounds of their health.

An application by the AMHP under this section has to be based on two medication recommendations, at least one of which is provided by a registered medical practitioner who is approved under section 12 of the MHA as having special experience in the diagnosis and treatment of mental disorders.

Once an application is made under this section, the patient can be treated without their consent. (See Chapter 6 to examine how medical treatment is given under the Act.) They can appeal to the Mental Health Tribunal within the first 14 days of their admission. (We discuss the Tribunal in more detail in Chapter 10.) The nearest relative has a right to be informed of the admission and their right to discharge the patient from hospital (discussed in Chapter 10).

Admission for treatment

If a patient does not need assessment in hospital, either because they have just been assessed under section 2, or because the details of the patient's mental disorder are known and it is clear what treatment is required, then the patient can be detained under section 3 of the Act. The legal grounds for detention are much stricter because the patient can be detained for a much longer period of time. They have to be suffering from a mental disorder of a nature *or* degree that makes it appropriate for them to receive treatment in hospital. Also it has to be 'necessary' for their health *or* safety *or* for the protection of others that the patient should receive such treatment. There also has to be appropriate treatment available for the patient and the two doctors have to state that this is available at the hospital to which the patient is going to be detained.

Again an application under this section has to be based on the medical recommendations of two doctors.

Once an application is made the patient can be treated without their consent. The period of detention can last up to six months, then it can be renewed by the responsible clinician (the approved clinician in charge of the patient's treatment) for another six months and then for a year at a time. As a result it is possible for a patient to remain detained under section 3 for a very long time. However, the period of detention cannot be renewed unless the grounds for detention continue to be met. The patient can appeal to the Tribunal once in each period of detention so within the first six months, then in the second six months and then once a year.

The nearest relative has the power to object to the AMHP making an application under this section. If they do object, then the patient cannot be detained. If the AMHP feels that the objection is unreasonable they can make an application to the County Court for the nearest relative to be displaced (MHA, s29). Also the nearest relative has the power to discharge the patient from hospital as for section 2. The responsible clinician can prevent the patient being discharged if they feel that the patient would be 'dangerous' to themselves or others if they were to be discharged. The criteria that it would be dangerous to discharge the patient is a much stricter test than the risk to the patient's health, safety or to others test required for the original detention. So the patient could still meet the grounds for detention in hospital but would have to be discharged from hospital following the nearest relative's order if the patient is not considered to be 'dangerous'. If the responsible clinician blocks the nearest relative discharge order then the nearest relative can appeal against this decision to the Mental Health Tribunal.

Emergency admission for assessment

This provision is set out in section 4 of the Act and can be used to admit a patient for assessment in an emergency, when there is not time to arrange for two doctors to attend. It is based on the recommendation of one doctor, who does not have to be section 12 approved. It can only be used in situations of 'urgent necessity' and only lasts for up to 72 hours. If a second doctor examines the patient within the 72 hours and provides a medical recommendation for detention under section 2 then the patient then becomes detained under section 2, and the 28 days runs from the day the patient arrived in hospital under the section 4. The patient cannot be treated without their consent, and while they can appeal to the Tribunal the section does not last long enough for a hearing to be arranged. However, if they were further detained under section 2 then the hearing would go ahead.

Conveying patients to hospital

Once the decision has been made by the AMHP and the two doctors that the patient needs to be detained in hospital, then the AMHP has to make their application based on the medical recommendation(s). They cannot do this until a bed has been found and the hospital has agreed to take the patient. Sometimes it can take quite some time to find the bed and the AMHP is left in an uncomfortable situation, having a patient who needs to be admitted to hospital and no bed being available. The AMHP has to manage this situation as best they can. They can end up being left alone with a patient if there are no relatives and the doctors have left. Therefore, if you know the patient, consider supporting the AMHP (and the patient) by staying until all the arrangements have been made to convey the patient to hospital. Also there may be practical arrangements that need to be made, such as getting clothes and toiletries together (if the patient is cooperative), and considering who is going to look after any children and/or pets. You may need to discuss with the AMHP who is best placed to make these arrangements. Once the bed has been secured, the application can be completed and the patient then becomes what is called 'liable to be detained'. They are not yet detained as they have not arrived at the hospital but they are in legal custody and not free to do what they like. The completed application and the medical recommendation(s) are sufficient legal authority for the hospital to detain the patient. All the hospital has to do is check the papers are properly completed and accept the patient; they then become detained by the hospital.

Once the papers have been completed, the AMHP has to arrange for the patient to be conveyed to hospital. This is usually by ambulance and it can take some time for it to arrive. The AMHP has the power to use restraint if necessary to get the patient into the ambulance and on to the hospital. However, most AMHPs are not trained in the use of restraint and in any event, it would be very difficult for one person to restrain a patient on their own. The AMHP can also authorise other professionals to use restraint such as ambulance staff or the police. Ambulance staff are often uncomfortable in using anything more then minimal force to encourage a resisting patient to go into the ambulance but they are usually very patient, caring and understanding, and can be very good at persuading a patient to go with them. It does help that they have a uniform that is associated with a caring profession. However, if persistent attempts at persuasion or minimal force do not work, then the police may have to be called to assist. Each area should have joint policies in place between the local authority, health services, police and ambulance services which set out how detained patients should be conveyed to hospital (MHA Code, paras 14.80, 17.22–17.28).

The AMHP is also responsible for making arrangements for the patient's property to be secured, any children to be taken care of and any pets to be looked after (MHA Code, para 14.88), an issue we explore in the following activity.

Sudden admission to hospital

Imagine that you are not at home and the decision has been made that you need an urgent admission to hospital and there is no time to go home first. What arrangements would need to be made and who would be available to make them? Think about this in regard to the following areas of your life:

- *Your home, emptying the bins, fridge, etc. Making sure the bills are paid and your home is secure, etc.*

- *Your caring responsibilities. Who is going to look after your children, your pets or your parents? Who is going to do the shopping for your neighbour?*

- *Your relationships. Who will tell your children or your partner what is happening? What arrangements will need to be made for them to visit you? How are they going to know where you are and how to get to you?*

- *Your professional responsibilities. What information do you want your employer to know? Who is going to cover your work and how will they know what needs doing?*

- *Your social life. How will you maintain your social contacts? How will they find out what has happened to you? Do you want them to know?*

Imagine that you are working with a person who has just been detained in hospital after being picked up by the police. How will you help them deal with these issues?

Patients already in hospital

If a patient who is in hospital informally changes their mind and wants to leave hospital, and the staff of the hospital think it is necessary for them to remain in hospital, then section 5 of the Act can be used to 'hold' the patient in hospital until an assessment for either section 2 or section 3 can take place.

Section 5(2) allows for an in-patient be detained for up to 72 hours in order for an assessment for further detention to take place. This section applies if the doctor (or approved clinician) in charge of the treatment feels that an application under the Act needs to be made (section 2 or section 3). This section can be applied in a general hospital as well as a psychiatric hospital.

Section 5(4) only applies in the case of an in-patient receiving treatment for a mental disorder. It allows a registered (mental health or learning disability) nurse to hold a patient for up to six hours if the patient is suffering from a mental disorder of such a degree that it is necessary to immediately restrain them from leaving the hospital, and it is not possible to secure the attendance of a doctor (or approved clinician) to apply section 5(2) of the Act. If a doctor or approved clinician attends within the six hours and applies section 5(2), then the 72 hours run from the time the section 5(4) holding power began.

Patients detained or held under section 5 cannot be treated against their will and they cannot appeal to the Tribunal.

Warrant to enter, search for and remove patients

Most people who own their own home or have a tenancy have the right to control who is able to come into their home and who is not. If someone comes into your home without your permission or refuses to leave when you ask them to, they are committing the civil wrong (tort) of trespass. This also applies to an AMHP, doctors and other members of the assessing team who are seeking to carry out an assessment under the Mental Health Act. Therefore, the team can only enter the patient's home with their permission or the permission of another person who is also lawfully entitled to reside there. If permission is refused then the team cannot enter. If the team enter the property with permission and that permission is later withdrawn, then the team have to leave.

AMHPs do from time to time have to gain entry to a property where they suspect a mentally disordered patient is residing in order to carry out an assessment. Section 135(1) of the Act allows for an AMHP to apply to a magistrate (Justice of the Peace) for a warrant to enter private premises, search for, and if thought fit, remove a patient to a 'place of safety' (for up to 72 hours) in order to carry out an assessment. If the patient is living alone then the grounds for applying for the warrant are simply that the patient is unable to care for themselves. However, if they are not living alone the grounds are stricter. The AMHP has to believe that the patient is, or has been, ill-treated, neglected or kept otherwise than under proper control.

Once the AMHP has obtained the warrant, they need to secure the attendance of the police to execute the warrant. The AMHP also has to be present and so does at least one doctor. The AMHP will usually either try and get a key to the property, from a relative or a friend, or will ask for a locksmith to attend to gain entry and secure the property afterwards. Sometimes a locksmith cannot gain entry and then the police will have to use force to break through the door. As you can imagine this is something that everyone present will want to avoid so every effort will be made to persuade the patient to let the assessing team into the property. Once inside the property, the AMHP and the police need to make a decision whether they think it is appropriate to remove the patient to a place of safety. If you are present at a warrant being executed and the patient is removed, the AMHP may ask you to stay behind to ensure that the property is secured, especially if force has been used to gain entry. The warrant only authorises the police to enter, search for and if thought fit to remove the patient. It does not allow for the team to remain in the property without permission. If permission is given then it is likely that the assessment will take place in the property but the power to remove the person is still available if permission is withdrawn. An assessment under the Act will then usually take place as discussed above in order to decide if the person needs to be detained under section 2 or section 3.

A 'place of safety' is defined in section 135 as a registered care home, a hospital, a police station or any other suitable place that the occupier of which is willing to accept the person.

Mentally disordered people found in public places

Under section 136 of the Act a power is given to police officers to remove a person who they think is mentally disordered in a public place to a place of safety for assessment. The police officer has to be of the view that the person is in need of immediate need of care and control, and that it is necessary in the interests of the person or the protection of others to remove them to a place of safety (same as for section 135(1)). A public place for the purposes of this section is 'a place to which the public have access' and is not defined in the Act or the Code of Practice. However, Jones (2013: 1–1278) states that it probably includes:

- places to which the public have open access

- places to which the public have access on payment of a fee

- places to which the public have access at certain times of day

The person can be held at the place of safety for up to 72 hours from when they arrive. The purpose of this section is to enable the person to be examined by a doctor, interviewed by an AMHP, and for any arrangements to be made for their treatment or care. If on examination by the doctor, the person is not found to be mentally disordered at all, then they must be released. If they have a mental disorder, they need to be interviewed by an AMHP who will then decide if the person needs a further assessment to see if they need to be detained, admitted to hospital informally or if other arrangements need to be made to provide care or treatment to the person.

The Care Quality Commission (CQC) have found that police stations are too often being used as places of safety (2014: p67) and have stressed the need for the NHS to provide sufficient health-based places of safety along with sufficient staffing to avoid the need to use police stations. The MHA Code of Practice (para 16.38) states:

> A police station should not be used as a place of safety except in exceptional
> circumstances, for example it may be necessary to do so because the person's
> behaviour would pose an unmanageably high risk to other patients, staff or other users
> if the person were to be detained in a healthcare setting. A police station should not
> be used as the automatic second choice if there is no local health-based place of safety
> immediately available.

CASE STUDY

Sule

Sule's GP has contacted the AMHP service expressing concerns about Sule's mental health. Sule is a young man from West Africa studying medicine in the UK. He is in the third year of his course. Over the last few months he has become increasingly anxious and worried about his grades. He has been staying up all night completing assignments and has not been eating. He is now neglecting his self-care, something which his friends say is out of character as he normally prides himself on his appearance. He is expressing ideas that people are following him and trying to steal his work. His friends say that he is staying in his room and rarely comes out. He used to be a very sociable person. His GP has discussed getting help but Sule is refusing because he states that he will not be able to get a job as a doctor back home if people knew he had mental health problems. However, he says that he is finding the pressure of work too much but he cannot ask for help because he does not want his family to know he is having problems with his course.

The duty AMHP is thinking about whether or not to arrange an assessment under the MHA. What do you think the impact of the assessment on Sule could be, even if it is decided not to apply for his detention in hospital after the assessment?

Mental Capacity Act assessments

The circumstances and processes for carrying out assessments of a person's capacity to make a specific decision under the Mental Capacity Act are much less rigidly defined. The MCA has a much more flexible approach and, as we have already discussed, seeks to be an enabling piece of legislation. As a result it is much less mechanistic and bureaucratic than the MHA, with the possible exception of its DOLS provisions. As a result, the onus is on social workers, and other professionals, when working with vulnerable adults in making decisions about their care and/or treatment, to ensure that the provisions of the MCA are applied when required. While there is a presumption that a person has capacity to make a specific decision (MCA, s1(2)), if you have any doubt (MCA Code, para 4.34) that a person lacks the capacity to make the decision that you are discussing with them, you should satisfy yourself one way or the other before proceeding. How to assess capacity is discussed in Chapter 3. However, the Act states that assessments of capacity should not be made merely by reference to the person's age, their appearance or by making unjustified assumptions about their condition or behaviour (MCA, s2(3)).

If you are working with a person with regard to a specific decision, it is your responsibility to assess whether or not the person lacks the capacity to make that decision (MCA Code, para 4.38). You cannot ask someone else to make that assessment. The more complex the decision the more likely the need for a formal assessment of capacity and you may need another professional's opinion as to their capacity. But the final decision is still with the professional who is intending to make the decision, or carry out the action, on behalf of the person who lacks capacity (MCA Code, paras 4.43 and 4.54).

Once you have determined that the person lacks capacity to make the decision, you then need to decide what is in the person's best interests. We discuss this in Chapter 6.

CHAPTER SUMMARY

- Before making a referral to an approved mental health professional, social workers have to have considered if there is a less restrictive alternative to admission to hospital.

- Social workers should be familiar with local procedures when making a referral for an assessment under the Mental Health Act, including ensuring that they collate and provide as much information about the person and their family situation as possible.

- Social workers should make themselves available to support the person they are working with through the process of the assessment and admission to hospital if necessary.

- The Act allows for admission to hospital for assessment (section 2), for treatment (section 3) and in cases of an emergency (section 4).

- Section 135(1) allows for an AMHP to apply to court for a warrant to enter a person's property, by force if need be, to search for them and remove them in order to assess if they need to be admitted to hospital.

- The police have certain powers under section 136 to remove mentally disordered persons to a place of safety in order for them to be assessed further.

- The Mental Capacity Act has a more flexible approach to assessments, that depends on the decision in question at the material time.

FURTHER READING

Brown, R, Barber, P and Martin, D (2009) *The Mental Capacity Act 2005: A Guide for Practice*, 2nd edition. Exeter: Learning Matters.

Chapters 5 and 6 discuss how to assess a person's capacity to make a specific decision and what needs to be considered when making a decision in their best interests.

Department of Health (2015) *Mental Health Act 1983: Code of Practice*. London: TSO.

Chapters 13 to 16 of the Code talk about how people should be assessed under the Act.

Chapter 6
Providing care

This chapter will help you to develop the following capabilities from the Professional Capabilities Framework:

- **Professionalism**
  Identify and behave as a professional social worker committed to professional development.

- **Values and ethics**
  Apply social work ethical principles and values to guide professional practice.

- **Rights, justice and economic well-being**
  Advance human rights and promote social justice and economic well-being.

- **Knowledge**
  Apply the knowledge of social sciences, law and social work practice theory.

- **Intervention and skills**
  Use judgement and authority to intervene with individuals, families and communities to promote independence, provide support and prevent harm, neglect and abuse.

It will also help you develop the following National Occupational Standards for Social Work in Wales:

- **Maintain professional accountability**
  SW 1: Maintain an up-to-date knowledge and evidence base for social work practice.

- **Practise professional social work**
  SW 4: Exercise professional judgement in social work.

- **Promote engagement and participation**
  SW 9: Engage people in social work practice.
  SW 10: Support people to participate in decision-making processes.
  SW 11: Advocate on behalf of people.

Introduction

Once a person is subject to compulsory care or treatment, or care to which they were not able to consent, it does not mean that those professionals providing the care can do what they like. Compulsory care is provided within a framework of law and subject to guidance from Codes of Practice. In this chapter we will examine how care and treatment is provided to patients detained under the Mental Health Act (MHA) and people who lack the capacity to consent to the provision of care and/or treatment in hospital and other settings. This is not a time when social workers should feel that they are on the sidelines whilst the doctors, nurses and other professionals get on with their jobs. This is a time when people are at their most vulnerable, and the law provides them with certain rights and protections. Also, the Codes of Practice set out in no uncertain terms how care should be provided and how professionals should attempt to involve people in decisions about their care and treatment. Many approved mental health professionals (AMHPs) do not understand these provisions in detail so it is important you understand how to support patients with regard to their medical treatment, especially if it is under compulsion. Social work has a long history of seeking to work collaboratively with vulnerable adults in order to reduce the risk that they may present to themselves or others. In this chapter we will examine how you can apply your social work values and skills to people who are either being treated against their will or are not able to consent to care being provided to them. We have explored the guiding principles of both the Mental Health Act 1983 and the Mental Capacity Act 2005 in Chapter 5; in this chapter we will examine how you as a social worker can work within a multi-disciplinary team to ensure that these values and principles are applied to the care of vulnerable adults.

We will start by considering the position of patients detained under the Mental Health Act 1983. The rights of detained patients will be examined along with the duties of the hospital to provide information to patients and relatives. We will look at the role of the independent mental health advocate and how they can support patients to understand their rights and to exercise them. Medical treatment under the MHA will be examined as well as the specific rules governing certain medical treatments. The role of care planning in providing compulsory care will be examined, as well as exploring how patients should be involved in drawing up plans about their care.

When it comes to exploring the provision of care under the provisions of the Mental Capacity Act (MCA), we will start with decision making in a person's best interests, how this is done and what factors need to be considered. We will then examine the use of restraint to provide care to understand when it can and cannot be used. The role of the independent mental capacity advocate in best interests decision making will be explored. We will end the chapter by looking at how people can make decisions about how care should be provided to them at some future time when they lack the capacity.

The provision of compulsory care in hospital

In the previous chapter we considered the process by which a person becomes detained in hospital under the Mental Health Act. Once the patient arrives at the hospital and the application by the approved mental health professional is accepted, they become a detained patient and the hospital managers become the detaining authority. The Mental Health Act Code of Practice (MHA Code) states that it is the NHS trust who manage the hospital who are the hospital managers for the purposes of the Act, and it is the registered manager who is the hospital manager in the case of an independent hospital (para 37.2).

As the detaining authority, it is the hospital managers who have the primary responsibility for seeing that the requirements of the Act are followed. These responsibilities are usually delegated to individuals or groups of individuals within the hospital as set out in the hospital's policies and procedures. The MHA Code (para 37.3) states that these responsibilities include:

- Ensuring that patients are only detained as the Act allows, i.e. that the detention of each patient is lawful.

- Making sure that patients are fully informed of, and supported in exercising their rights as set out in the Act.

- The care and treatment of detained patients accord fully with the provisions of the Act.

Social workers have a duty to uphold the rights of people who use services (Health and Care Professions Council Standards of Proficiency for Social Workers in England, para 2.7, and Code of Practice for Social Care Workers in Wales, para 3.1) and as such, you need to understand the rights of detained patients and the legal framework within which hospital managers operate so that you can ensure that the treatment is lawful and that patients are able to exercise their rights.

The rights of the detained patient

The MHA Code of Practice gives detailed guidance about the rights of detained patients and what information should be given to them. Hospital managers usually delegate this duty to registered nurses on the ward treating the patient. The requirement to give information about their rights equally applies to patients on community treatment orders (CTOs) and we will consider this in more detail in Chapter 7. It is important to note that the MHA Code (para 4.10) talks about hospital managers ensuring that, as far as possible, patients can understand their rights. Mere giving of information is not sufficient.

Patients need to be informed of the provisions under which they are detained (section 2, section 3, etc.), including the maximum length of the current period of detention. Patients also need to be told the reasons for detention and the grounds under which they have been detained. AMHPs making applications to detain patients in hospital need to leave an outline report at the hospital and write a full report for their employers (MHA Code, paras 14.93 and 14.95). One of the purposes of these reports is to explain the reasons for the patient's detention. If you are working with a person who is detained in hospital it is important that you read the AMHP's report so that you can understand the reasons for the detention and are able to support the person in understanding why they are in hospital. A patient cannot effectively challenge the grounds for their detention unless they understand why they have been detained in the first place.

Patients should be informed of the rights of their nearest relative to discharge them and what can happen if their responsible clinician (the professional in charge of the patient's treatment) does not agree with that decision (see Chapter 10).

With regard to treatment for their mental disorder under the Act, patients need to be told:

- the circumstances in which they can be treated without their consent and when they can refuse treatment;
- the role of second opinion appointed doctors (SOADs) and the situation in which they need to become involved in decisions about their treatment;
- the rules regarding electroconvulsive therapy (ECT) if relevant (MHA Code, para 4.20).

We will discuss these provisions later in this chapter.

Patients have the right to seek a review of their detention. They should be informed of the right of the responsible clinician and the hospital managers to discharge them (except for restricted patients, see Chapter 8). They need to be informed of their right to ask the hospital managers to discharge them and that the hospital managers must consider discharging them when their detention is renewed. The patient also should be informed of their right to apply to the Mental Health Tribunal to discharge them, the rights, in limited circumstances, of their nearest relative to apply to the Tribunal, the role of the Tribunal and how they can apply to the Tribunal (MHA Code, para 4.21). We will examine the role of the Mental Health Tribunal in Chapter 10.

The role of the Care Quality Commission (CQC) needs to be explained to patients, as does their right to meet with Mental Health Act reviewers (CQC staff who visit detained patients) in private. They should also be informed of their right to make a complaint to the CQC as well as to the hospital managers (MHA Code, paras 4.25–4.26).

Detained patients can have post sent by them withheld if the person to whom it is addressed asks the hospital managers to do so, and they need to be informed of this (MHA Code, para 4.27).

ACTIVITY 6.1

Exercising rights

Imagine you are meeting with a patient who has just been detained in hospital for the first time. You have been given the task of explaining to them their rights. They are upset, distressed and scared about what is happening to them. Think about your meeting with them. What information are you going to give them and how are you going to explain it to them? Think about the specific rights as discussed in this chapter and how you can explain these to the patient. It may help for you to role-play this situation with a fellow student, a colleague or a friend/relative.

The patient tells you that they wish to appeal against their detention. How do they go about this? How are you going to help them with their appeal?

As we have seen, these rights are extensive and it can be difficult for a well person to remember them, never mind a detained patient who is mentally disordered. As we have seen from Activity 6.1, explaining rights to a patient is not always easy to do. The hospital managers need to ensure that these rights are given orally and in writing. They need to ensure that all the information is given in a way that the patient understands (MHA Code, para 4.10), as well as making sure that patients are regularly reminded about their rights. The CQC has been critical of the ability of hospitals to explain rights to their patients:

> However, there was no improvement in evidence of patients' rights being explained to them. In the last two years we have not seen adequate evidence of discussions with patients about their rights in at least one in 10 wards.

(CQC, 2014)

We can see that it can be all too easy for detained patients not to be fully aware of their rights, and if they are, they may not be assisted to exercise these rights. Also, as Hale (2010: p211) states, while there is no legal duty to do so, the MHA Code states that hospital managers need to make sure that informal patients are informed of their rights, otherwise there is a risk of unlawful detention. Therefore, it is important that social workers working with these patients endeavour to ensure that they are able to understand their rights and exercise them if they so wish.

Independent mental health advocate

One of the changes brought about by the Mental Health Act 2007 amendments to the 1983 Act is the duty to provide access to independent mental health advocates (IMHAs) (MHA 1983, s130A). Only certain detained patients are eligible for support from an IMHA, but IMHA services should not replace other advocacy and support services that are available to patients. The patients who are not eligible for IMHA support are those who are being held on short-term powers including section 4, section 5 or people in a place of safety under sections 135 or 136 (MHA Code, para 6.9).

The support provided by the IMHA includes helping detained patients to obtain and understand information about: their rights under the Act and the rights that other people have in relation to them (e.g. their nearest relative); the legal provisions under which they are detained; the restrictions and conditions that may apply to them; any medical treatment they are receiving or which is being proposed, the reasons for that treatment and the legal authority for providing that treatment, including safeguards (MHA Code, para 6.12). An IMHA is more than about providing and understanding information. They also should help patients to exercise their rights, which can include representing them in their conversations with their clinical team.

Interestingly, the Code (paras 6.23–6.24) states that AMHPs and responsible clinicians should consider requesting an IMHA to visit a detained patient if they think that the patient might benefit from the support of an IMHA and is unable or unlikely to request help from an IMHA themselves, after first discussing it with the patient. The provision of IMHA services and the access to such support varies significantly from hospital to hospital or even from ward to ward in the same hospital. Well commissioned IMHA services will visit wards on a regular basis and make themselves known to newly detained patients, offering their services. In other cases, the IMHA will only attend if they receive a referral, which will depend on the ability of the patient to contact the IMHA or on the nurses contacting them on the patient's behalf.

Therefore, it is important that you understand how IMHA services are provided at the hospital in which your patient is detained and that you discuss with them if they want to speak to an IMHA or not.

An IMHA has the right to meet the patient in private and should be able to attend meetings between patients and professionals when asked to do so by patients. However, there are limits on the ability of the IMHA to access records and confidential information on patients. If the patient consents then the IMHA can see their records. If they lack the capacity to make this decision then the hospital can grant access to the records only if it is appropriate and relevant to the help to be provided by the IMHA (see MHA Code, paras 6.30–6.38, for more details).

As with the rights of detained patients discussed above, the social worker that is working with any detained patient needs to consider the right of access to an IMHA and support the patient in accessing this service if they so wish. Also, if you are of the view that a patient would benefit from speaking to an IMHA and they are not able to request this themselves, you should consider asking the AMHP or responsible clinician to request an IMHA to visit.

Medical treatment

Before going on to examine the provision of medical treatment under the MHA, it is necessary to revisit the fundamental principle of valid consent, discussed in Chapter 2. Before a person can be given medical treatment, they need to consent to it. Without this consent any medical treatment could amount to a criminal offence, a civil wrong or violate the person's rights under the European Convention on Human Rights. However, there are exceptions to this fundamental principle. One is that medical treatment can be imposed on a person without their consent and even in the face of their outright refusal under the Mental Health Act 1983. Another is that in the case of a person who does not have the medical capacity to consent, care and/or treatment can be provided under the Mental Capacity Act 2005, which will be discussed later in this chapter.

Just because a patient's consent is not required in specific circumstances under the MHA, it does not mean that a patient should not be involved in discussions regarding their medical treatment. The MHA Code (paras 24.40–24.44) states that the patient's consent should still be sought before treatment is given, wherever possible, and that their consent or refusal should be recorded in their notes. If a patient changes their mind and withdraws their consent, the medical treatment should be reviewed by the clinician in charge of the treatment before deciding whether to impose the treatment or to discontinue it. The Care Quality Commission, when carrying out its duty to visit detained patients in hospital, found that in a significant proportion of records there is no recorded discussion with the patient regarding consent when they are first admitted to hospital and after the first three months (CQC, 2014: p53). The significance of the first three months will be discussed later.

The MHA Code of Practice (para 4.8) states that wherever possible patients should be engaged in the process of reaching decisions that affect their care and treatment under the Act. If the clinical team makes a decision that is contrary to the patient's wishes, that decision and the reason for it should be explained to the patient in a way that they understand.

We can see that social workers can have a very powerful role here. As the CQC have found, some doctors are not very good at discussing medical treatment with their patients before the treatment starts and do not even try and get the consent of the patient when they are capable of consenting. As well as ensuring that the patient you are working with understands and is able to exercise their rights, you have a role to play with regard to medical treatment. You should be considering what conversations have taken place with the patient, how their views have been considered as well as what they know and understand about their medical treatment. If a decision has been made against the patient's wishes, you need to ensure that the clinical team have explained to the patient the reasons for this decision.

Medical treatment under the MHA is not just about medication, or procedures like electroconvulsive therapy (ECT); it includes nursing care, psychological intervention, rehabilitation and care (MHA 1983, s145(1)). Also, the purpose of the medical treatment must be to alleviate or prevent a worsening of a mental disorder or one or more of its symptoms or manifestations (MHA 1983, s145(4)). If the medical treatment is not for a mental disorder, it cannot be imposed under the Act. The medical treatment can be provided to treat not only the mental disorder itself, but also its symptoms or manifestations. These can include physical conditions that have caused the mental disorder such as infections, strokes, brain tumours, etc. as well as physical conditions that are caused by the mental disorder, such as self-poisoning by a drug overdose, or the wounds caused by self-harm by cutting. However, medical treatment for conditions that have arisen indirectly (such as neglecting management of diabetes or other medical conditions) is not included, although treatment could be provided via the MCA if the person lacks the capacity to make this decision.

We have discussed the importance of gaining consent where possible, and examined the Mental Health Act's definition of medical treatment and its purpose. We now need to move on to consider what medical treatment can be imposed in what circumstances. Section 63 of the Act states:

> The consent of the patient shall not be required for any medical treatment given to him for the mental disorder from which he is suffering, not being a form of treatment to which section 57, 58 or 58A above applies, if the treatment is given by or under the direction of the approved clinician in charge of the treatment.

The approved clinician in charge of the treatment is usually the responsible clinician (RC), which in most cases will be a consultant psychiatrist who has undertaken training to become an approved clinician.

Not all patients detained under the Act can be treated against their will. We have discussed this when examining the specific detention provisions, but the basic rule is that patients detained under short-term provisions (72 hours or less) cannot have treatment imposed against their will.

There are special safeguards in place for treatments that come under sections 57, 58 or 58A. Section 58 applies to treatment with medication after the three months from when medication was first administered. Section 58A applies to ECT and section 57 to surgery to destroy the functioning of brain tissue and the surgical implantation of hormones to reduce male sex drive. We will consider these safeguards in turn as well as the exceptions for treatment needed in an emergency (MHA 1983, s62).

For the first three months, medication can be given to a patient without consent and without any additional safeguards. After three months, medication can only be given if the patient consents or a second opinion appointed doctor (SOAD) states that the treatment should be given. If the RC wants to continue with medication after three months they need to certify in writing that the patient understands the nature, purpose and likely effects of the treatment and has consented to it (MHA 1983, s58(3)(a)). The RC needs to record this on the relevant statutory form (forms are set out in the MHA 1983 regulations) also with specific details of the medication to be administered. Also the Code of Practice requires that the RC records the relevant discussions with the patient regarding their medical treatment and their capacity to consent in their notes (para 25.17). However, if the patient refuses to give consent or is not able to understand the nature, purpose and likely effects of the treatment, then the RC needs to request that a SOAD attends to examine the patient. A second opinion appointed doctor is employed by the CQC and provides important safeguards for the patient in that they need to agree that medical treatment is appropriate before it can be provided. A SOAD needs to examine the patient, and discuss the case with two professionals involved in the patient's treatment, before deciding that either the patient effectively does not have the capacity to consent or if they do, that they are refusing. They record their decision on a statutory form along with the details of the medication that can be prescribed by the RC. After the first three months, only medication that is listed on the relevant statutory form can be given to the patient. Any medication that is not on one of these forms cannot lawfully be given to the patient unless it is for a physical disorder or section 62 applies.

Section 58A applies to electroconvulsive therapy. ECT is a controversial treatment but it is used to treat severe mental disorders – usually severe depression where the patient's life is at risk. An electrical current is passed through the brain to induce an epileptic fit (Royal College of Psychiatrists, 2014). Because of the concerns about the side effects of this treatment, extra safeguards were put in place with the implementation of the changes in the Mental Health Act 2007. ECT cannot now be given to an adult who has capacity to consent and is refusing the treatment (apart from in an emergency under section 62). In order for ECT to be given to an adult they have to consent and the RC (or SOAD) has to have certified that the patient understands the purpose, nature and likely effects of the treatment and has consented. If the adult patient does not have the capacity to consent and needs ECT, a SOAD has to attend and examine the patient, certify that the patient cannot understand the nature, purpose and likely effects of the treatment, that the treatment is appropriate and there is no valid and applicable advance decision refusing ECT. Therefore, if a patient, when they have capacity, makes an advance decision to refuse ECT, then that decision is binding on the clinicians even when the patient is detained under the MHA, and ECT cannot be given. An advance decision to refuse medication or other medical treatment under the Act is not binding but the clinicians should have regard to the wishes of the patient (MHA Code, para 9.9). We will discuss advance decisions in more detail later in the chapter. There are slightly different rules governing the giving of ECT to children and young people.

Section 57 is unusual in that it applies to informal patients as well as those detained under the MHA. It provides that psychosurgery or surgical implantation of hormones cannot be given unless:

- the patient consents;
- a SOAD and two other people appointed by the CQC certify that the patient is able to consent and has done so;
- the SOAD certifies that it is appropriate that the treatment is given to the patient.

As a result, patients who lack capacity cannot be given these sorts of treatment at all.

In an emergency there are exceptions to these safeguards and these are set out in section 62 of the Act. The section 62 provisions can appear to be a bit complicated at first glance as there are different rules for medication and for ECT. However, treatment under section 62 can only continue for as long as it is required and then only if it is 'immediately necessary' (MHA 1983, s62(1)(a)). This test is a strict test which requires more than that the treatment required is merely urgent (MHA Code, para 25.40). Medical treatment can only be provided if it is immediately necessary to:

- save the patient's life;
- prevent a serious deterioration of the patient's condition, and the treatment does not have unfavourable physical or psychological consequences which cannot be reversed;
- alleviate serious suffering by the patient, and the treatment does not have unfavourable physical or psychological consequences which cannot be reversed and does not entail significant physical hazard; or
- prevent patients behaving violently or being a danger to themselves or others, and the treatment represents the minimum interference necessary for that purpose, does not have unfavourable physical or psychological consequences which cannot be reversed and does not entail significant physical hazard.

(MHA Code, para 25.38)

If the treatment is ECT then the first two categories are the only ones that apply, and in effect it means that ECT can only be given in an emergency if the patient's life is at risk, as ECT in some cases can have some irreversible side effects such as memory loss (Royal College of Psychiatrists, 2014).

Care planning

We have already discussed the empowerment and involvement principle in Chapter 4 which states that patients should be given the opportunity wherever possible to be involved in planning, developing and reviewing their own treatment and care. The

CQC found that in 2012/13 there was evidence that patients were involved in planning their care in 57 per cent of cases and that the care plans took account of the patients' views in 61 per cent of cases (CQC, 2014: p27). This still leaves a significant proportion of cases where there was no recorded involvement or recording of views. The CQC have criticised the lack of patient-centred care planning that it has seen during Mental Health Act monitoring visits (CQC, 2014: p28). The MHA Code of Practice states that wherever possible the whole treatment plan should be discussed with the patient (para 24.49). It is clear that patients are not always involved in discussions about their treatment and care and where this does take place, their views are not always considered and documented. One of your roles as a social worker, visiting a person that you are working with who is detained in hospital, is to ensure that they are involved as far as possible in the planning of their care and that their views are taken into account.

ACTIVITY **6.2**

Patients communicating their views

Think about a case where you worked with a person to express their views to a medical professional involved in their care. This may have been to a general practitioner, during an outpatient appointment, or as part of care planning in an inpatient stay, whether for a mental disorder or not. How did you work with the person to enable them to think about what they wanted to happen to them? How did you work with the person to support them to communicate their views to the medical professional who is making decisions about them? What did you do when you felt the professionals were not taking sufficient account of the person's views? How did you facilitate the medical professional explaining to the person the reasons for the decisions made when they were not able to accommodate the person's wishes?

The provision of care to people who lack capacity to make decisions

The provisions of Part IV of the Mental Health Act 1983 only apply to patients who are detained under the Act, i.e. it is status-based. This means that the provisions of the Act only apply if you have the status of being detained under the Act. The Mental Capacity Act 2005 is not status-based, it is considered to be a function-based statute, i.e. you come within its provisions as a function of not having the capacity to make a particular decision. As a result, assessing capacity and making decisions about what care needs to be provided if the person lacks capacity needs to be done on a case by case and a day by day basis, often by different professionals for different decisions and different types of treatment and/or care. It is important to remember that issues of capacity are decision specific, and making a blanket decision that a person is 'incapacitated' has no basis in law.

Given that the MCA could potentially apply to a wide range of people in a wide range of settings under the care of a wide range of professionals, it is important that professionals continually check out whether the person they are caring for comes within its provisions. It is much easier when it comes to the MHA because the person's status under the Act determines whether or not that Act applies.

We have considered the process of assessing capacity in Chapters 3 and 5. Only when it has been found that the person lacks the capacity to make a particular decision can the professional concerned then move on to think about how that decision should be made.

Best interests decision making

As we have already discussed the best interests principle is a fundamental statutory principle that underpins how the MCA should be implemented:

> An act done, or decision made, under this Act for or on behalf of a person who lacks capacity must be done, or made, in his best interests.

> (MCA 2005, s1(5))

This principle covers all aspects of certain areas of a person's life, including financial decisions, personal welfare and healthcare decision making. It also applies to anyone making decisions on behalf or acting under the provisions of the MCA including informal carers, relatives, and health and social care professionals (MCA Code, para 5.2).

Best interests decision making only covers certain decisions as section 5(1) of the MCA only provides protection for actions carried out in relation to care or treatment. So if the decision is not regarding a person's care or treatment it does not come within the provisions of the MCA. The MCA Code of Practice sets out the sort of decisions that can be made in a person's best interests under section 5 of the Act:

Personal care

- helping with washing, dressing or personal hygiene
- helping with eating and drinking
- helping with communication
- helping with mobility
- helping someone take part in education, social or leisure activities
- going into a person's home to drop off shopping or to see if they are alright
- doing the shopping or buying necessary goods with the person's money
- arranging household services
- providing services that help around the home
- undertaking actions related to community care services (for example, day care, residential accommodation or nursing care)
- helping someone to move home

Healthcare and treatment

- carrying out diagnostic examinations and tests (to identify an illness, condition or other problem)

- providing professional medical, dental and similar treatment

- giving medication

- taking someone to hospital for assessment or treatment

- providing nursing care (whether in hospital or in the community)

- carrying out any other necessary medical procedures (for example, taking a blood sample) or therapies (for example, physiotherapy or chiropody)

- providing care in an emergency

(MCA Code, para 6.5)

One exception to the best interest principle is where the person has made an advance decision to refuse medical treatment. If the decision is one that is covered by the advance decision and it is valid, the advance decision has to be followed. This will be discussed in more detail later in the chapter.

So how do you make a decision in a person's best interests when you have determined that they lack the capacity to make that decision? The Mental Capacity Act 2005 does not define the term 'best interests' because this covers a wide range of decisions by a wide range of people concerned with a person's care. However, the Act does provide a checklist of factors that need to be considered before a best interest decision is made. The MCA Code of Practice stresses that this checklist is only a starting point and there well may be more factors that you need to take into account (para 5.6). The checklist is to be found in section 4 of the Act and it is helpfully summarised in the introduction to Chapter 5 of the MCA Code of Practice:

- do whatever is possible to permit and encourage the person to take part, or to improve their ability to take part, in making the decision

- try to identify all the things that the person who lacks capacity would take into account if they were making the decision or acting for themselves

- try to find out the views of the person who lacks capacity, including:

  o the person's past and present wishes and feelings – these may have been expressed verbally, in writing or through behaviour or habits

  o any beliefs and values (e.g. religious, cultural, moral or political) that would be likely to influence the decision in question

  o any other factors the person themselves would be likely to consider if they were making the decision or acting for themselves

- not make assumptions about someone's best interests simply on the basis of the person's age, appearance, condition or behaviour

- consider whether the person is likely to regain capacity (e.g. after receiving medical treatment). If so, can the decision wait until then?

- not be motivated in any way by a desire to bring about the person's death. They should not make assumptions about the person's quality of life

- if it is practical and appropriate to do so, consult other people for their views about the person's best interests and to see if they have any information about the person's wishes and feelings, beliefs and values. In particular, try to consult:

  o anyone previously named by the person as someone to be consulted on either the decision in question or on similar issues

  o anyone engaged in caring for the person

  o close relatives, friends or others who take an interest in the person's welfare

  o any attorney appointed under a Lasting Power of Attorney or Enduring Power of Attorney made by the person

  o any deputy appointed by the Court of Protection to make decisions for the person

- For decisions about major medical treatment or where the person should live and where there is no-one who fits into any of the above categories, an Independent Mental Capacity Advocate (IMCA) must be consulted

- When consulting, remember that the person who lacks the capacity to make the decision or act for themselves still has a right to keep their affairs private – so it would not be right to share every piece of information with everyone

- see if there are other options that may be less restrictive of the person's rights

- weigh up all of these factors in order to work out what is in the person's best interests

This list may appear overwhelming at first but the actions are easy to understand and do sit easily within your social work value base and your training in working with vulnerable adults.

ACTIVITY 6.3

Making a best interests decision

You are involved in the case of a person whose situation has deteriorated to the point where serious consideration is being given to whether or not the person needs to be admitted into residential care. You have undertaken a detailed capacity assessment that clearly documents your reasons for finding that the person is not able to make decisions about their treatment or care. However, they are able to express their wishes and their relatives are able to explain their previous wishes and feelings. Think about what factors you would consider when making your decision about whether or not it is in their best interests to be admitted into residential care. What factors, if they were different, would cause you to make a different decision?

It is important to note that the more serious the decision, the more rigorously this process must be followed and documented. For example the demands on an informal carer helping a person to change from their night clothes to their day clothes are much less rigorous than a clinical team making the decision that a person in hospital needs to move into a care home and not return home. The following case study helps to consider how to apply the requirements for best interest decision making in practice.

Unlike the MHA there are no forms that you need to complete to document a capacity assessment or best interests decision, but you are encouraged to document your decisions because this provides authority for you to act, and serves as a protection from liability as you can evidence how you have complied with the law (Brown et al., 2009: p67).

CASE STUDY

Prashanti

Prashanti is a woman in her early 60s. She is a first generation immigrant from India. Her husband has recently died from cancer. She lives in a large city in the family house, which is in need of some repair. Her daughter lives nearby and has a young family. Prashanti has a long history of depression but the family have rarely sought professional help. Her late husband provided much of the care that Prashanti needs and her daughter provided some support around the needs of her young family. Her GP has referred Prashanti to local mental health services because she is worried about her mental state and is concerned that she is starting to develop some form of dementia. Prashanti has always been reluctant to accept help from outside the family. She has turned away professionals in the past. However, her daughter is struggling to provide sufficient care for her mother. Prashanti is losing weight and she is not keeping herself clean. Neighbours have found her wandering the street in her nightclothes and have had to return her home. Her daughter states that her mother has always enjoyed living in that house and does not want to move elsewhere.

You have assessed her capacity to make decisions with regard to her care needs and she is not able to understand her needs as well as the risks she faces without support. She states that she is fine and that she does not need help. You feel that she lacks the capacity to make decisions about her care. Think about what care Prashanti needs and how this is going to be provided in the least restrictive way possible. How are you going to balance her wishes with her need for care?

Use of restraint to provide care

There are situations that require a person who lacks capacity to make decisions about keeping themselves safe to be restrained to prevent them coming to harm. This is provided for in section 6 of the Act. This states that you cannot restrain a person who lacks capacity unless you reasonably believe that it is necessary to restrain the person in order to prevent harm, and that the restraint is a proportionate response to the likelihood of the person suffering harm and the seriousness of the harm. We can see from this that the restraint can only be applied if the person is going to come to harm. It cannot be used to prevent them harming others unless they too would come to harm. Also, the restraint needs to be the minimum necessary for the shortest possible time to keep the person safe.

Restraint is defined as the use of force or the threat of the use of force to secure the doing of an act which the person is resisting, or restricts the person's movement whether they are resisting or not (MCA 2005, s6(4)(a) and s6(4)(b)). This is quite a wide definition and is more than actually laying hands on someone. Restricting a person to an area of their home or care home could come within this definition of restraint and can only be used if the grounds discussed above are met and for the shortest possible time. It is important to note that in order for the restraint to be lawful it cannot be so severe that it amounts to a deprivation of liberty (this will be discussed in Chapter 9).

Independent mental capacity advocate

An independent mental capacity advocate (IMCA) provides important safeguards with regard to decision making on behalf of a person who lacks capacity in certain situations. IMCAs also have certain roles to play under the Deprivation of Liberty Safeguards (DOLS) and we will discuss these in Chapter 9.

An IMCA must be appointed when a person lacks the capacity to make certain decisions and they do not have anyone else to support them (apart from paid staff) when the following are under consideration (MCA Code, para 10.3):

- An NHS body is proposing providing serious medical treatment.

- An NHS body or a local authority is proposing to arrange accommodation (or a change of accommodation) in hospital or care home and the person will be in hospital for more than 28 days or they will stay in a care home for more than eight weeks.

An IMCA may be appointed to support someone who lacks capacity to make decisions concerning reviews of care (if there is no-one else available to be consulted) and in adult safeguarding cases even if there are family, friends or others involved.

The role of the IMCA is to be independent, provide support for the person who lacks capacity, represent the person in discussions with professionals to work out if the decision is in their best interests or not, provide information to help work out what is in the person's best interests and raise questions and challenge decisions which do not appear to be in the person's best interests (MCA Code, para 10.4).

If you, as a social worker, are working with a person who lacks the capacity to make decisions about going into residential care for more than eight weeks (or hospital for more than 28 days), and you know that they do not have someone to support them (who is not paid), then you must ensure that an IMCA is appointed. The duty to appoint the IMCA will be with the local authority that is proposing a move into a care home, or the NHS body that is proposing the admission to hospital for treatment or transfer to a nursing home.

Advance decision making

An advance decision is a decision made by a person (who has reached the age of 18) to refuse specified medical treatment at a point in the future when they no longer have the capacity to make that decision. This decision only relates to a refusal of medical treatment; it cannot be used to demand specific treatment or care. However, people can make a request or express wishes in advance but these are not binding on professionals in the same way as an advance decision. However, professionals have to take account of wishes expressed in advance as part of the best interest checklist.

In order for an advance decision to be binding on the professionals providing the treatment or care (i.e. it has to be followed), it has to be both valid and applicable. In order for the advance decision to be valid and applicable, the MCA s25 states that the person has to:

- have reached the age of 18;

- have had the capacity to make that advance decision at the time they made it;

- and, if it relates to life-sustaining treatment, it must be in writing, signed and witnessed, and state clearly that the decision applies even if life is at risk.

An advance decision is not valid if the person has withdrawn it at a time they had capacity to do so, they have appointed a Lasting Power of Attorney after the advance decision was made (Lasting Power of Attorney will be discussed in Chapter 10), or the person has done anything inconsistent with the advance decision remaining their fixed decision. An example of the latter may be an advance decision to refuse a blood transfusion, but the person later consents to a blood transfusion when they have capacity and forgets to withdraw the advance decision.

The advance decision has to be applicable to the treatment in question and as such it can be difficult for professionals to decide if the person had that particular treatment in mind when they made the decision. Also, it can be difficult for a person to plan ahead and make decisions about what treatment they do not want to receive in the future if they do not know what treatment might be in consideration. It may be much easier to consider these matters in the early stages of an illness as the person may have a clearer idea of what they do not want to happen to them. As a social worker working with a person who faces the prospect of losing the capacity to make decisions for themselves, it is important that you support the person to make a valid and applicable advance decision if that is their wish.

CHAPTER SUMMARY

- Once a patient is detained in hospital under the Mental Health Act, they have certain rights. Social workers should be familiar with these rights and ensure that anyone they are working with understands them and is able to exercise them if they so wish.

- Most detained patients are entitled to have support from an independent mental health advocate.

- Staff should always gain the consent of patients to their medical treatment where possible.

- Staff should follow the patient's wishes if possible, and document when they have departed from these wishes as well as explain to the patient their reasons.

- There are provisions within the Act for treatment to be imposed against a patient's will. These are governed by specific rules and procedures.

- The Mental Capacity Act allows for decisions to be made on behalf of people who lack capacity only as long as it is in their best interests.

- Social workers should be familiar with what decisions can be made in a person's best interests and the best interests checklist.

- Restraint can be used under the Mental Capacity Act but only when it complies with the requirement of the Act.

- Independent mental capacity advocates provide an important safeguard for people who lack the capacity to make certain decisions. Social workers need to understand when an IMCA must be involved and when they should be involved.

FURTHER READING

Department of Constitutional Affairs (2007) *Mental Capacity Act 2005 Code of Practice*. London: TSO.

Chapter 5 discusses what is involved in making a best interests decision.

Department of Health (2015) *Mental Health Act 1983: Code of Practice*. London: TSO.

Chapter 4 discusses what information should be provided to patients detained under the Act. Chapter 6 talks about the role of the independent mental health advocates, and Chapter 8 about the need to protect the privacy, dignity and safety of detained patients.

Chapter 7
Care outside of hospital

Introduction

We now need to explore the provisions within the Mental Health Act 1983 which relate to the discharge of patients from hospital and care outside of the hospital setting. The use of compulsion outside of hospital is controversial but the Act does provide for certain powers to be exercised over patients in order to provide care and as a result avoid readmission to hospital. These powers will be explored in this chapter. The power of the responsible clinician (RC) to grant leave of absence to a patient from the hospital in which they are detained is a key part of the care and treatment. Leave of absence is much more than just giving the patient a break from the ward; it is a vital part of their recovery and rehabilitation. All patients who have been detained on longer-term sections are entitled to aftercare under section 117 of the Act, and services have a duty to provide the aftercare that the patient needs. However, section 117 aftercare, on its own, cannot impose care against the patient's wishes. There are a couple of provisions that can apply to patients which can subject them to varying degrees of compulsion in the community: the guardianship order and the community treatment order (CTO).

If you as a social worker are working with adults who experience mental disorders, it is likely that you will be working with adults who are subject to these provisions. This chapter seeks to help you gain a greater understanding of these provisions and how they might apply to the service users you are working with. In considering the use of compulsion in the community there is a key tension between care and control, as we discussed in Chapter 4. You have a key role in promoting independence and empowerment, keeping patients informed of their rights and supporting them in exercising these rights. Your knowledge of these provisions will support you in expressing your views to other professionals about the appropriateness or otherwise of imposing these provisions on patients in the community.

Section 17 leave of absence

Section 17 of the Mental Health Act gives the responsible clinician (RC) the power to grant a patient leave of absence from the hospital. This is often known as section 17 leave. A patient who is detained in hospital cannot lawfully leave the hospital unless they have been given section 17 leave by their RC. There are certain patients who cannot be given section 17 leave (those detained under sections 35, 36 or 38, which are discussed in Chapter 8), and restricted patients (sections 41, 45A and 49, again discussed in Chapter 8) cannot be granted leave without the permission of the Ministry of Justice. There does not need to be a formal procedure to grant leave for patients to move around the hospital and the grounds.

The MHA Code states that leave of absence can be an important part of a detained patient's care plan but that there are risks attached to the granting of leave. The Code (para 27.10) requires that RCs consider the following before granting leave:

- consider the benefits and any risks to the patient's health and safety of granting or refusing leave
- consider the benefits of granting leave for facilitating the patient's recovery
- balance these benefits against any risks that the leave may pose for the protection of other people (either generally or particular people)
- consider any conditions which should be attached to the leave, e.g. requiring the patient not to visit particular places or persons
- be aware of any child protection and child welfare issues in granting leave
- take account of the patient's wishes, and those of carers, friends and others who may be involved in any planned leave of absence

- consider what support the patient would require during their leave of absence and whether it can be provided

- ensure that any community services that will need to provide support for the patient during the leave are involved in the planning of the leave, and that they know the leave dates and times and any conditions placed on the patient during their leave

- ensure that the patient is aware of any contingency plans put in place for their support, including what they should do if they think they need to return to hospital early

- liaise with any relevant agencies

- undertake risk assessments and put in place any necessary safeguards, and

- (in the case of Part III patients, see chapters 22 and 40) consider whether there are any issues relating to victims which impact on whether leave should be granted and the conditions to which it should be subject

Section 17 leave can have conditions attached. These always include whether the patient needs to be escorted, accompanied or can be unescorted. It is likely that at first leave will be escorted with the patient then moving to accompanied leave and then unescorted leave. Escorted leave is where the patient has leave but remains in the custody of a member of staff of the hospital (or someone authorised in writing by the hospital managers). This will usually be a nurse or a healthcare worker from the ward but occasionally this can be community staff if they are so authorised. After a period of escorted leave the RC may come to the view that whilst the patient no longer needs to be in the custody of hospital staff, the patient needs to be accompanied whilst out on leave. A friend or relative can then accompany the patient whilst on leave. As a social worker you may be asked to accompany a patient on section 17 leave and it can be an important part of your work with that patient in preparing them for discharge from hospital. Before you agree to accompany a patient, be sure to check with the RC whether or not the patient is your 'legal custody' (MHA Code, para 27.27) and if so what that means. If you are escorting a patient on leave, you need to either be on the staff of the hospital or have written authorisation from the hospital managers. If you are taking a patient out of the hospital on leave you need to make sure that you understand your legal responsibilities and what you need to do if the patient absconds. This has to be set out in the hospital's absent without leave policy (MHA Code, paras 28.11–22.23). Section 17 leave needs to be recorded on a standard form and a patient should have a copy of this form as should any relatives or professionals accompanying the patient.

Whilst a patient is on section 17 leave they are 'liable to be detained' and they are still subject to Part IV of the Act (discussed in Chapter 6) so they can have treatment against their will. These provisions can be useful if the patient is going on longer-term leave to see how they respond to support, in a care home or supported living placement, for example. If a patient does not comply with the conditions imposed by the RC they can be recalled from leave and returned to hospital. If they refuse to return they are 'unlawfully at large' and force can be used to return them to the hospital. However, if they are in their own property and refuse to grant access, staff of the hospital will need to apply to the local magistrates for a warrant to enter the property and remove the patient under section 135(2) of the Act.

If the RC is considering granting leave for more than seven days, they need to consider whether the use of a community treatment order is more appropriate (MHA, s17(2A)).

Section 117 aftercare

This section of the Act requires clinical commissioning groups (CCG) (Local Health Boards in Wales) and local social services authorities (LSSA) to provide aftercare to certain groups of patients. Patients who are entitled to section 117 aftercare are those who are detained under section 3 and on section 17 leave, or those who have been detained under section 3, section 37 (hospital order), section 45A (transfer and limitation direction), section 47 or 48 (transfer directions). The duty to provide aftercare is triggered once the person ceases to be detained, i.e. they are discharged from detention.

Section 117 has been amended by the Care Act 2014, which came into force on 1 April 2015. The new section 117 now defines aftercare for the first time and simplifies which LSSA is responsible for providing aftercare. The Care Act 2014 inserts a new sub-section 6 into section 117 which defines aftercare services as having the following purposes:

(a) meeting a need arising from or related to the person's mental disorder; and

(b) reducing the risk of a deterioration of the person's mental condition (and, accordingly, reducing the risk of the person requiring admission to a hospital again for treatment for mental disorder).

Prior to these amendments, aftercare was not defined, which often led to disputes between patients and local authorities about which services came within section 117. This is a significant issue because patients cannot be charged for services provided under section 117, whereas they can be charged for services which are provided in order to meet needs not related to a person's mental disorder. It is important to note that section 117 provides specific duty to provide aftercare to a specific group of people and it is separate from the more wide-ranging duties that a local authority has to provide services under the Care Act 2014. It is possible for a person to have some services provided under section 117 of the Mental Health Act, while other services for other social care needs not related to their mental disorder are provided under the Care Act. The person cannot be charged for section 117 MHA services, but could be charged for Care Act services.

Section 117 states that the duty to provide aftercare services rests with the CCG and LSSA where the patient was 'ordinarily resident' before being detained in hospital. This is a change from the previous requirement that the patient be 'resident', which is a much looser test than 'ordinarily resident'. What it means to be 'ordinarily resident' is not set out in statute but is defined in case law and is known as the Shah test (*R v Barnet LBC ex parte Shah* [1983] 1 All ER 226).

Ordinary residence is established if there is a regular habitual mode of life in a particular place 'for the time being', 'whether of short or long duration', the continuity of which has persisted apart from temporary or occasional absences. The only provisos are that the residence must be voluntary and adopted for 'a settled purpose'.

There can be disputes between one local authority and another over who has section 117 responsibility. The amended section 117 in sub-section 4 gives powers to the Secretary of State or Welsh Ministers to resolve these disputes. Prior to these amendments, the only way to resolve these disputes was to go to court.

However, when the responsibility to provide aftercare comes to an end has still not been defined. The MHA Code (para 33.20) states that the duty to provide aftercare services exists until both the CCG and the LSSA are satisfied that the patient no longer requires them. Therefore, if the patient requires support from either health or social services then the duty to provide aftercare continues. So there may be a situation where a person does not receive services from secondary mental health services but is just being prescribed medication under the supervision of their GP. As long as it meets a need arising from the mental disorder and it reduces the risk of deterioration, then the person is still entitled to section 117 aftercare.

Patients are not under any obligation to accept the aftercare services they are offered and if they refuse such services they are still entitled to section 117 aftercare if they change their minds (MHA Code, para 33.24). Services cannot use a patient's refusal as grounds to discharge the patient from section 117 aftercare.

Planning for discharge from hospital needs to start as soon as possible after admission and needs to include how the CCG and LSSA are going to carry out their duty to provide aftercare. This is a statutory duty on these public authorities and not something that they can avoid. The MHA Code (para 34.19) sets out what should be included in an assessment of the patient's needs and wishes. These include:

- continuing mental healthcare, whether in the community or on an out-patient basis
- the psychological needs of the patient and, where appropriate, of their family and carers
- physical healthcare
- daytime activities or employment
- appropriate accommodation
- identified risks and safety issues
- any specific needs arising from, for example, co-existing physical disability, sensory impairment, learning disability or autistic spectrum disorder
- any specific needs arising from drug, alcohol or substance misuse (if relevant)
- any parenting or caring needs
- social, cultural or spiritual needs
- counselling and personal support

- assistance in welfare rights and managing finances

- the involvement of authorities and agencies in a different area, if the patient is not going to live locally

- the involvement of other agencies, for example the probation service or voluntary organisations

- for a restricted patient, the conditions which the Secretary of State for Justice or the Tribunal has imposed or is likely to impose on their conditional discharge, and

- contingency plans (should the patient's mental health deteriorate) and crisis contact details

It is very likely if you are working with a person who has a mental disorder that you will be involved in discharge planning, including the provision of section 117 after-care. You may be one of the professionals involved in a person's care on discharge, or you may have overall responsibility for coordinating a person's care plan. This is usually via the care planning process called the Care Programme Approach (CPA), and the professional who is responsible for coordinating the care plans is called the care coordinator (Department of Health, 2008). As such you bring your social work values and perspectives to the discharge planning process: you need to ensure that the patient's wishes and feelings are taken into account, consider the views of relatives, and ensure that the social and cultural needs of the patient are met, as well as the medical needs. You will also need to ensure that any assessments and services that the person is entitled to under the Care Act 2014 are carried out and put in place. Once the section 117 discharge plan is in place, you will need to ensure that it is implemented, especially if you are the one responsible for coordinating the care plan. Also, section 117 plans need to be regularly reviewed, and if you are the care coordinator you will be responsible for ensuring that these reviews take place. The shortest review period is usually three months, but periods of six months to a year are more common. Reviews should take place at least yearly and more frequently if the needs of the patient are likely to change.

Guardianship

Section 7 of the Mental Health Act provides for a patient to be received into guardianship. The Code (para 30.2) states that the purpose of guardianship is to enable patients to receive care outside of hospital when it cannot be provided without the use of compulsory powers. Whilst guardianship has not been a popular option for local authorities and its use continues to decline, it is useful to know about its provisions, as it may be a useful option when considering the need for a legal framework to provide care to a patient in the community.

A guardian is usually a local social services authority, but it could be someone else who is approved by the LSSA and such a person is known as a 'private guardian'. When a patient is received into guardianship, the guardian has three specific powers with regard to the patient (MHA, s8(1)):

- require the patient to reside at a place specified by the guardian

- require the patient to attend for treatment, occupation, education or training

- require access to the patient to be given, at any place where the patient is residing to any doctor, approved mental health professional, or other relevant person

As a result of these powers, guardianship can be a useful option that is less restrictive than a standard authorisation under Deprivation of Liberty Safeguards (DOLS) (discussed in Chapter 9) or a community treatment order. The MHA Code (para 30.4) states:

> Guardianship therefore provides an authoritative framework for working with a patient, with a minimum of constraint, to achieve as independent a life as possible within the community. Where it is used, it should be part of the patient's overall care plan.

There are things that guardianship cannot do. It cannot authorise the deprivation of the patient's liberty in any setting. Therefore, if the care being provided at the place where the patient is required to reside amounts to a deprivation of liberty, it has to be authorised via a separate legal procedure. If the person has to reside in a care home this could be done via DOLS, or if the person has to reside in a supported living or independent living setting then this will have to be via the Court of Protection. Also, guardianship cannot authorise medical treatment. The patient has to either consent to the medical treatment, if they are able to give such valid consent, or if they lack capacity to make this decision, the person providing the treatment has to decide that it is in the patient's best interests.

Guardianship is most often used to enable a patient to reside at a place specified by the guardianship in cases where the patient is refusing or resisting. There is a power to take a patient to the place they are required to live in the first place and to return them there if they leave (MHA, s18) and this power can be enforced. The Code (para 30.30) states that this power may be used to discourage them from: living somewhere unsuitable, breaking off contact with services, leaving the area before arrangements can be made or sleeping rough. If the patient is not resisting and lacks capacity to make a decision about where they should reside, the Code (para 30.11) encourages the Mental Capacity Act provisions (MCA, s5) to be used instead.

The process of assessing and applying for a person to be received into guardianship is very similar to the process of applying for detention in hospital. The grounds for a guardianship application are that the patient is suffering from a mental disorder of a nature *or* degree which warrants reception into guardianship; *and* it is necessary in the interests of their welfare *or* for the protection of others they are received into guardianship (MHA, s7(2)). The patient cannot be received into guardianship unless they are at least 16 years old. Also the learning disability qualification applies to guardianship so a person with a learning disability cannot be received into guardianship unless the learning disability is associated with seriously irresponsible or abnormally aggressive conduct. Like applications for admission to hospital, a guardianship application is made by an approved mental health professional based on the recommendations of two doctors, one of whom must be approved under section 12 of the Act. Also, like applications for detention under section 3 of the Act, a patient's nearest relative can object to a guardianship application, which prevents the patient being received into guardianship. The nearest relative has the power to discharge the patient from guardianship. Instead of the AMHP applying to the hospital, in guardianship cases the AMHP makes the application to the local social services authority. If an LSSA is going to be the guardian then the application needs to be to that LSSA. If the guardian is going to be a private guardian, the application needs to be made to the LSSA in the area where the guardian lives.

In practice a guardianship application is based on wider considerations of the care plan that is required for the patient. The Code (para 30.20) states that an application for guardianship should be accompanied by a comprehensive multi-disciplinary care plan. Therefore, the starting point for discussions about guardianship should be in a care-planning meeting involving the whole of the clinical team. As a result you may be involved in discussions about whether or not guardianship would be the most appropriate way of providing the care that the patient needs. As you can see, the guardian has significant powers over the patient. These powers should only be used if they are required and there is not a least restrictive option. Your social work values, as discussed in Chapter 4, come into play here to ensure that guardianship is the most appropriate way forward for the patient and that the patient understands, as far as possible, the implications of being received into guardianship. However, you should also consider that guardianship might be a less restrictive and more appropriate option than other options that the clinical team may be considering such as a standard authorisation under DOLS or a community treatment order.

A guardianship order can be imposed by the courts under section 37 of the Act as an alternative to a hospital order (see Chapter 8). The court cannot do this unless the grounds are met and the LSSA or the named guardian is willing to act as guardian.

ACTIVITY **7.1**

Guardianship policy

Look up and read your local authority's policy on admitting people into guardianship. If you felt that a person you were working with needed to be admitted into guardianship, how would you go about this? What factors would you have to consider and with whom would you need to discuss this?

Community treatment order

The power to impose a community treatment order (CTO) was one of the changes brought in by the Mental Health Act 2007. It inserted sections 17A to 17G into the

Act. Hale (2010: p233) argues that over the years psychiatrists have pressed for ways to ensure that detained patients keep up with their medication and do not get lost on leaving hospital. The CTO was devised as a way of achieving this and preventing what is called the 'revolving door patient' where the patient is frequently readmitted to hospital under the Act because they have stopped their medication and become unwell again. Community treatment orders are not without their critics. Some argue that they are not effective (Burns et al., 2013) while others feel that they infringe human rights, namely Article 8 of the European Convention on Human Rights, and significant concerns have been expressed about the over-representation of people from Black and Minority Ethnic communities on CTOs (Mental Health Alliance, 2010).

The MHA Code of Practice (para 29.5) states that the purpose of a CTO is to allow suitable patients to be safely treated in the community rather than under detention in hospital and to provide a way to help prevent relapse. The main feature of the CTO is that it gives the responsible clinician (RC) the power to recall a patient to hospital for treatment if required. As a result the CTO is a health-based provision whilst guardianship is based within social services. When consideration is given to using one of these provisions in the community, the decision making needs to focus on the needs of the patient and which provision is best suited to meet these needs. A CTO is much more concerned with medical treatment and medication whilst guardianship is focused on broader welfare concerns.

Unlike guardianship, a CTO can only be used on a patient who is already detained in hospital on either section 3 (admission for treatment) or an unrestricted Part III patient (see Chapter 8), usually section 37 hospital order patients. There is no lower age limit for a CTO. A CTO can only be imposed if the patient meets the following grounds (s17A(5)):

- the patient is suffering from a mental disorder of a nature or degree which makes it appropriate for them to receive medical treatment
- it is necessary for the patient's health or safety or for the protection of others that the patient should receive such treatment
- subject to the patient being liable to be recalled as mentioned below, such treatment can be provided without the patient continuing to be detained in a hospital
- it is necessary that the responsible clinician should be able to exercise the power under section 17E(1) of the Act to recall the patient to hospital and
- appropriate medical treatment is available for the patient

The main reason for a CTO to be considered is that the power of recall is needed. If the power of recall is not required then a CTO is not appropriate. The MHA Code (para 29.45) states that the recall power is intended to provide a means to respond to evidence of relapse or high-risk behaviour relating to mental disorder before the situation becomes critical and leads to the patient or others being harmed. The power of recall can be used earlier in a relapsing situation, where there is not sufficient time to arrange an assessment for detention under section 2 or section 3, or where the recall is needed to give the treatment that the patient is refusing and then the patient can be returned to the community.

The process of making the community treatment order is very different to applications for detention and guardianship. With a CTO, the responsible clinician is the applicant and the AMHP has to agree that the CTO is appropriate and agree with the RC which conditions should be imposed on the order. Strangely there is no requirement that the AMHP interviews or even knows the patient but in most cases the AMHP would have to interview the patient to satisfy themselves that the CTO is appropriate and obtain the patient's views. The AMHP has an important role here because the CTO cannot go ahead unless they agree to it. A CTO lasts for six months in the first instance and then can be extended for another six months and then yearly. An AMHP has to agree to the extension.

The CTO must include conditions with which the patient has to comply whilst on the CTO. There are two types of conditions: mandatory conditions and discretionary conditions. The mandatory conditions are imposed on every CTO patient and they require the patient to make themselves available for medical examination in two situations: when an extension of the CTO is being considered and when a second opinion appointed doctor (SOAD) needs to examine the patient. If a patient does not comply with these conditions then they can be recalled to hospital without any evidence of any need for hospital treatment. The RC and AMHP can also agree a range of other conditions that they think are necessary or appropriate. However, the MHA Code (para 29.28) states that such conditions can only be imposed to:

- ensure that the patient receives medical treatment for mental disorder
- prevent a risk of harm to the patient's health or safety as a result of mental disorder, and
- protect other people from a similar risk of harm

If the condition does not seek to achieve one of these aims then it should not be imposed. Conditions should be kept to a minimum, restrict the patient's liberty as little as possible and be clearly and precisely set out so the patient can easily understand what is expected of them and how they are able to comply with these conditions. You may well be involved in discussions in care planning meetings about the use of a CTO, and as such you can express your views about the appropriateness of such an order and make sure that the conditions are the minimum possible and the patient can understand them. If the patient cannot understand the conditions, how are they going to be able to comply with them?

If it is decided to recall the patient, for other reasons than not complying with a mandatory condition, this needs to be based on the need for the patient to have treatment in hospital. Not complying with a discretionary condition is not in itself sufficient grounds for recall. The Code (para 29.46) states that the RC may recall the patient to hospital for treatment if they need to receive that treatment as either an inpatient or outpatient and there would be a risk of harm to their health or safety or to other people if the patient was not recalled. So a recall does not necessary lead to the patient being admitted. They could be recalled to receive outpatient treatment such as the giving of medication for example. Once a patient is recalled they come within Part IV of the Act and can be given treatment against their will. This cannot be done in the community. A recall can last for up to 72 hours and if the RC feels that the patient needs to remain in hospital beyond this time, they need to arrange for the CTO to be revoked. The revocation involves the RC and an AMHP who both have to agree that the patient again needs to be admitted to hospital for medical treatment under the Act and that it is appropriate to revoke the CTO. Once the order is revoked the patient becomes detained once again under the original section 3 or section 37.

As for most patients subject to the Mental Health Act, a CTO patient is entitled to apply to the Mental Health Tribunal and the hospital managers (discussed in Chapter 10). Also if the patient was originally detained under section 3, the nearest relative can order the patient to be discharged from the CTO. However, if the original detention was under Part III of the Act, then the nearest relative cannot discharge the CTO but they can apply to the Tribunal to do so. CTO patients are also entitled to the services of an independent mental health advocate (see Chapter 6).

CASE STUDY

Catherine

Catherine has a history of involvement in mental health services. She has a long-standing diagnosis of bipolar disorder. She has periods when she is high in mood, resulting in her spending money she does not have, being overactive and not sleeping, as well as believing she has superpowers. She is currently in hospital under section 3 of the Mental Health Act 1983. This is her third admission this year and they follow a similar pattern. When Catherine is well, she does not like to take medication as it reminds her of her mental illness. However, when she stops taking her medication she quickly relapses and her mood becomes high again. Her responsible clinician and her social worker are keen to try and stop this cycle of admissions. Catherine wants to get back to work. She does not want to be made subject to a community treatment order (CTO) as she feels that when she gets out of hospital she does not want to be reminded that she has a mental disorder and wants to get on with her life.

You are Catherine's social worker. What factors do you think are important when it comes to the responsible clinician and the AMHP considering a CTO? Do you think a CTO would be helpful in Catherine's case?

CHAPTER SUMMARY

- A detained patient can be granted leave from hospital under section 17 of the Act.

- Patients detained under longer-term sections are entitled to free aftercare once they have been discharged from hospital under section 117.

- Patients can be subject to compulsion in the community in certain circumstances. These include patients subject to guardianship and community treatment orders.

Department of Health (2015) *Mental Health Act 1983: Code of Practice*. London: TSO.

Chapters 29 and 30 discuss community treatment orders and guardianship.

Part III

Other provisions and safeguards

Chapter 8

Mentally disordered offenders

Introduction

As a social worker working with vulnerable adults, you will from time to time come across situations where the person you are working with comes into contact with the criminal justice system. They may be accused of committing a criminal offence and may find themselves in police custody, put before the courts and may even end up in prison. This chapter will give you an overview of the interface between the criminal justice system and mental health law in order to equip you to better support those who are accused of criminal offences and have mental health problems. This area of law is complex and we will be considering a number of statutes. However, you are not expected to have more than a basic understanding of these provisions. Even approved mental health professionals (AMHP) usually only have a basic grounding in this area of law unless they specialise in forensic mental health work. A basic level of understanding of the law in this area will give you confidence in your interactions with criminal justice agencies: the police, magistrates and crown courts, prisons, probation services and the Ministry of Justice.

We will start by examining the principles underpinning Government policies towards mentally disordered offenders. We will then look at what happens in the police station if the person who has been arrested appears to have a mental disorder, with a particular focus on the role of the appropriate adult. We will then look at the powers of the courts as an alternative to conviction and those available prior to the person being convicted. We will then examine the options available to the courts on a finding of guilt when it comes to sentencing the offender. Before going on to consider the supervision of mentally disordered offenders in the community on discharge or release, we will examine the powers available in respect of sentenced prisoners.

Lord Bradley, in his review of people with mental health problems or learning disabilities who come into contact with the criminal justice system, defined offenders with mental health problems as:

> those who come into contact with the criminal justice system because they have committed, or are suspected of committing, a criminal offence, and who may be acutely or chronically mentally ill.

> (Bradley, 2009: p17)

Throughout this chapter we will be using the term 'mentally disordered offender' (MDO) to describe this group of people. We have discussed the terms used to describe people who experience mental distress in Chapter 2 and the term mentally disordered offender is subject to similar critique. However, for ease of use and legal accuracy we will be using this term.

Underpinning principles

As Fennell (2011: p214) states, Government policy with regard to mentally disordered offenders rests on three basic principles. The first is that mentally disordered suspects should be subject to special safeguards surrounding their treatment in custody, since they may be particularly prone to making false confessions. The second is that mentally disordered offenders should be, where possible, diverted away from the criminal justice system and into the health and social care system. The third has come to dominate discussions around the reform of mental health law since the early 1990s and this is that the public require protection against the risk posed by mentally disordered people.

This policy of diversion has been described by Bradley (2009: p16) as a process where offenders' mental health needs are assessed as early as possible following their contact with the criminal justice system in order to inform decisions about where the person is best placed to receive treatment, taking into account the need to protect the public, the need to keep the person safe and the need to provide punishment for an offence. Fennell argues that two ideas underpin this policy of diversion: first, that the presence of a mental disorder may reduce the person's culpability for the offence; and second, that they will be vulnerable to suicide and self-harm (2011: p214).

Culpability is defined as 'responsibility for a fault or wrong: blame' (Oxford Dictionaries, 2014). For most criminal offences there are two elements that have to be shown to exist before a person can be found guilty: that the person did the act (the 'actus reus', which is Latin for guilty act) also known as the physical element and that they intended to commit the offence (the 'mens rea', which is Latin for guilty mind) also known as the mental element (The Free Legal Dictionary, 2014). As we can see, the presence of a mental disorder can affect the required mental element required for a person to be convicted of an offence. This may mean that their culpability for the offence may be reduced or even extinguished completely. We will be considering the effects of reduced or extinguished culpability as we move through the chapter.

In the police station

Once a person has been arrested in connection with an offence and brought to a police station they come within the provisions of the Police and Criminal Evidence Act 1984 (PACE). This Act provides special protection for mentally disordered or mentally vulnerable persons whilst they are in police custody. This Act is supported by several Codes of Practice but the most relevant one for our considerations is Code C (Home Office, 2014). The Code states that the custody officer (the police officer in charge of the custody suite) must make sure that a detainee (the arrested person) receives appropriate clinical attention as soon as reasonably practicable if they appear to be suffering from a mental disorder (PACE Code C, para 9.5). Following the Bradley report (2009) there has been an increase in the number of mental health professionals available in police stations. The role of these professionals is to ensure that the mental health needs of detainees are met, and to advise police on appropriate diversions if they are of the view that the person is acutely mentally disordered. The police also have access to doctors (usually called forensic medical examiners (FMEs)) who are usually general practitioners who are on call to attend the police station when required. FMEs have to deal with all the medical needs of detainees and not all have any specialist skills or training in mental health.

The Mental Health Act Code of Practice (MHA Code) states:

> Wherever possible, people who appear to police custody officers or the court to be mentally disordered should have their treatment needs considered at the earliest possible opportunity, by the liaison and diversion service . . . where there is one or other professionals providing healthcare in police custody. Vulnerable people may be at greatest risk of self-harm while in custody. Prompt access to specialist treatment may

prevent significant deterioration in their condition and is likely to assist in a speedier justice process, helping to avoid longer-term harm or detention in an unsuitable environment.

(MHA Code, para 22.4)

Fitness to be interviewed

If the custody officer is concerned about a detainee's mental health they have to assess whether a detainee is fit to be interviewed in connection with the alleged offence. Annex G to PACE Code C sets out the responsibilities of police officers and healthcare professionals in making these sorts of decisions. It may be that conducting an interview could significantly harm the detainee's physical or mental health or it may be that the evidence obtained in the interview might be considered by a court to be unreliable because of the detainee's physical or mental state. If the custody officer has concerns about the fitness of the detainee to be interviewed, they will usually ask a health professional (usually the FME) to assess. The health professional will advise the custody officer if they think that the detainee is fit to be interviewed or not but the decision rests with the custody officer.

If the custody officer feels that the interview cannot go ahead then the police cannot take any further action at this time with regard to the alleged offence. However, there may be considerable concerns about the detainee's mental state and the potential risk that they present to themselves or others. As they are unfit to be interviewed the person cannot proceed within the criminal justice system. If they need urgent mental healthcare then hospital admission will have to be considered. The MHA Code (para 22.3) states:

> People who are subject to criminal proceedings have the same rights to psychiatric assessment and treatment as anyone else. Any person who is in police or prison custody or before the courts charged with a criminal offence and who is in need of medical treatment for mental disorder should be considered for admission to hospital where the criteria are met. Wherever possible, alternatives to custody for vulnerable individuals should be considered taking into account all information about the person's health needs, including assessment by the liaison and diversion service where one is available.

There is nothing to prevent a person arrested in connection with an offence being admitted to hospital informally (MHA 1983, s131) if they have the capacity to consent to such an admission. However, if the person has been arrested for a serious offence and there is considered be a risk to the public, the custody officer may have concerns about the person being in hospital informally. The custody officer does have the power to put conditions on the granting of bail (PACE, s30A), which may include a condition to reside in the hospital, and the person will have to understand this condition before consenting to informal admission. However, the hospital may not be content to have such conditions imposed as this may interfere with the clinical judgement of the doctor in charge of the patient's treatment.

However, if the person lacks capacity to consent to admission to hospital, informal admission using section 5 of the Mental Capacity Act 2005 (MCA) could be problematic, especially if the primary reason for admission is to prevent harm to others as the MCA only provides powers to prevent harm to the person themselves, or if the police are considering a bail condition to reside at the hospital as this might constitute a deprivation of liberty (Article 5 European Convention on Human Rights) which cannot be authorised by the MCA. If there are such concerns about the level of risk that the person presents, it is very likely that the custody officer or the FME will request an assessment under the Mental Health Act 1983. We have discussed this process in detail in Chapter 5 and the considerations of the AMHP and the doctors are much the same as for any other assessment under the Act. As we will see, if the person requires admission to hospital under the MHA at this stage in the criminal justice process, the only way that this can be done is via Part II of the Act (sections 2, 3 or 4).

ACTIVITY *8.1*

Providing information and confidentiality

You are working with a person who has just been arrested with regard to an allegation that they committed an assault. You do not know about the circumstances of the alleged assault and as far as you know, they have not committed any previous offences. However, you do know that this person has problems with their temper and impulse control. You have been working with them to address these issues. What information, if any, do you give the police? Do you need to get the person's permission? When would you breach the person's confidentiality and what are your legal grounds for doing so?

Appropriate adult

Just because a detainee is mentally disordered or mentally vulnerable it does not automatically follow that they will not be fit to be interviewed in connection with an alleged offence. However, if the custody officer has 'any doubt' about the mental state or capacity of a detainee, that detainee should be treated as mentally vulnerable and an appropriate adult called (PACE Code C, note 1G). As a social worker working with vulnerable adults it is very likely that you will be called to be an appropriate adult in a police station, either in respect of a person you are working with or while on 'duty'. It is important that any professional undertaking the role of an appropriate adult has sufficient training before undertaking that role.

An appropriate adult does not have to be a professional: it can be a relative, although PACE Code C (note 1D) prefers it to be a person trained or experienced in the care of vulnerable adults. However, if the detainee prefers a relative or objects to the professional, their wishes, if practicable, should be respected. It is important for the professional appropriate adult to understand that they are not subject to legal privilege (PACE Code C, note 1E) so what is said to the appropriate adult by the detainee may have to be disclosed to the police. The appropriate adult should ask the detainee not to discuss any aspects of the alleged offence with them outside of the formal interviews with the police. Also, certain people should not be an appropriate adult, e.g. if they are suspected to be involved in the offence, the victim, a witness, involved in the investigation, or received admissions prior to attending to act as the appropriate adult (PACE Code C, note 1B). Therefore, if you have had any conversations with the detainee prior to the interview (even prior to the arrest) about the alleged offence, you may be compromised as an appropriate adult and you should consider asking someone else to act. If you are concerned about the appropriateness of acting especially in view of conversations you may have had with the detainee, you should seek legal advice via your employer's legal team.

There is no legal duty on local authorities to provide appropriate adults, as the duty is on the police to ensure that they are present when a mentally vulnerable adult is detained in a police station. Currently there is no statutory basis for the provision of appropriate adult services for vulnerable adults. This is something that the National Appropriate Adult Network (2014) is arguing for.

While the role of the appropriate adult is not defined in statute, it can be gleaned from understanding what is stated in PACE Code C. The detainee has to be informed that the role of the appropriate adult includes giving advice and assistance and that they can consult privately with the appropriate adult at any time (PACE Code C, para 3.18). Also the police have to explain to the appropriate adult that their role is to:

- not act simply as an observer
- advise the person being questioned
- observe whether or not the interview is being conducted properly and fairly
- facilitate communication with the person being interviewed

(PACE Code C, para 11.17)

The appropriate adult is required to attend the police station where the person is detained and they should be given information about the grounds for detaining the suspect (PACE Code C, para 3.15). The appropriate adult should examine the custody record as soon as possible after they arrive at the police station (PACE Code C, para 2.4).

Even if the police have informed the detainee of their rights and the reason for them being held prior to the appropriate adult attending, this must be repeated in the presence of the appropriate adult (PACE Code C, para 3.17). The appropriate adult can overrule the detainee's refusal to seek legal advice and can request a solicitor on behalf of the detainee (PACE Code C, para 3.19).

A mentally vulnerable detainee cannot be interviewed without an appropriate adult present (PACE Code C, para 11.15). An appropriate adult can make representations to the police officer reviewing the detention to determine whether it is still necessary (PACE Code C, para 15.3). When the detainee is charged and/or bailed the appropriate adult needs to be present when information is given about charge and/or bail (PACE Code C, paras 16.1–16.6).

Issues in deciding who is best to act as an appropriate adult feature in the case study later in this chapter.

Powers prior to conviction or as an alternative to conviction

Once a suspect has been charged by the police with an offence or offences, they move on to be dealt with by the courts. The Mental Health Act 1983 sets out in Part III the powers available to the courts in respect of people who appear before them (called defendants or the accused). The powers available are in most cases different if the defendant is before the Magistrates' Court or the Crown Court. The magistrates' powers of sentencing are limited, so those accused of more serious offences will be transferred to the Crown Court for trial and sentencing.

However, before we go on to consider these provisions, we need briefly to examine what happens if the accused's mental disorder is so severe that they are not able to stand trial.

Fitness to stand trial

A person appearing before the Crown Court may be so disabled by their mental disorder that they are not fit to stand trial. This has nothing to do with their state of mind at the time of the alleged offence, but it is about the ability of the accused to take part in the court proceedings (Hale, 2010: p157). If the court has concerns about the ability of the defendant to take part in the proceedings, it may adjourn to enable the defendant to receive treatment so that they could recover to the point where they are fit to plead. This treatment could be provided via Part II of the Act or there are powers in Part III, which could compel treatment at this stage of the Crown Court proceedings that we will consider later.

However, if even after treatment in hospital the defendant is unable to stand trial, a procedure is set out in the Criminal Procedure (Insanity) Act 1964 as amended by the Criminal Procedure (Insanity and Unfitness to Plead) Act 1991 and the Domestic Violence Crime and Victims Act 2004. The Crown Court judge has to determine if the defendant is fit to plead (fit to stand trial) in the light of medical evidence. The judge, in deciding that the defendant is not fit to plead, needs to consider their ability to: plead to the charge(s), understand the course of the proceedings, instruct a lawyer, challenge a juror and understand the evidence. If the judge finds that the defendant is not fit, then there needs to be what is called a 'trial of the facts'. This is before a jury, and its role is to determine if the defendant did the act that they are charged with. This is to ensure that the defendant does not have a perfectly good defence before subjecting them to the options that the court can then impose. The jury finding that the defendant did the act is not the same as a conviction and as a result they are not formally found guilty of the offence. The jury is not required to consider the mental element of the offence, just the physical element. This can cause problems if the offence is one that has a significant mental element, e.g. for an offence of theft the person needs to have taken the item (actus reus) and to have intended to permanently deprive the rightful owner of the item (mens rea). Also, a defendant could have an absolute defence to a charge of murder if they were acting in self-defence, but in such a case it would be difficult for this to be known in the absence of evidence regarding the intent of the defendant in carrying out their actions. If the court finds that the person did the act, they can impose any of the following:

- a hospital order (with or without restrictions)
- a supervision and treatment order
- or an absolute discharge

Any hospital order and restriction order imposed by the court has the same meaning as orders imposed under sections 37 and 41 of the Mental Health Act 1983, and the grounds for admission under these sections need to have been met before the judge can make the order. We examine hospital orders in more detail later in the chapter.

There are different provisions if the person is in the Magistrates' Court, as the magistrates can make a hospital order in respect of a defendant who is not fit to plead, but where they are of the view that they did the act with which they are charged (MHA 1983, s37(3)). In both these situations it is important to note that the defendant is not convicted of an offence because they were not able to properly stand trial. In some cases, if the patient at a later time becomes fit to stand trial, they can be sent back to court to stand trial for the original offence.

Insanity defence

The above provisions relate to the defendant's mental state at the time of the trial, not at the time of the alleged offence. The defendant may argue in court that they were so mentally disordered at the time of the offence that they have no legal culpability for their actions. This is called the 'insanity defence' but is not used very often these days.

A person who is found to be 'insane' at the time of the alleged offence by the court may be found 'not guilty by reason of insanity' (Trial of Criminal Lunatics Act 1883, s2). This is called the 'special verdict' and it is an alternative to conviction, which means that the person does not have a formal finding of guilt by the court but neither have they been formally acquitted (Bartlett and Sandland, 2014: p361). The definition of insanity is still the same as set out in the M'Naughten case ((1843) 10 C & F 200). This is now considered to be a very dated definition of insanity that does not sit comfortably with current psychiatric opinion (Bartlett and Sandland, 2014: p362). The jury will still need to be satisfied that the accused did the act in a procedure similar to the 'trial of the facts'. Once a person has been found 'not guilty by reason of insanity' they can be made subject to the same provisions as a person found unfit to plead as discussed above.

Remands to hospital

A defendant who would otherwise be remanded in prison can be remanded in hospital instead. Where possible a court would remand a defendant on bail rather than in custody but the risks that the defendant poses may be such that custody is the only option.

Section 35 of the Mental Health Act 1983 gives the power to remand a defendant to hospital to enable a report to be produced on the defendant's mental disorder. This power could be used if it has not been possible to produce a report while the defendant is on bail, e.g. the defendant has not cooperated with requests to attend appointments with the psychiatrist tasked with producing the report. This power is available to both Magistrates' and Crown Courts. This section lasts initially for 28 days but can be extended by the court up to a maximum of 12 weeks. This, along with the fact that medical treatment cannot be imposed on the patient under Part IV of the Act, limits the usefulness of this section. If the doctor in charge of the treatment needs to enforce treatment then they will have to consider using Part II of the Act (sections 2 or 3) alongside section 35.

If the court wishes to remand a defendant in hospital for medical treatment, this can be done under section 36. The grounds are the same as for those for detention under section 3 of the Act. However, this power is only available to the Crown Court and it is an alternative to a remand in prison. Patients remanded under this section can be treated against their will, but the same time limits as section 35 apply, potentially limiting the usefulness of this section to the courts.

Power of the Secretary of State to transfer from prison to hospital

If a defendant has been remanded in prison awaiting trial or sentence, then the Secretary of State for Justice has the power under section 48 to direct the transfer of a prisoner to hospital. The grounds are again similar to those for section 3. The need for hospital treatment has to be urgent. They can be treated against their will. This section lasts until the defendant next appears in court but can continue until the court finishes with them either by discontinuing the case, an acquittal or a finding of guilt and then being sentenced.

In each of these three sections, the patient cannot appeal to the Mental Health Tribunal as they are still under the jurisdiction of the courts.

Powers on conviction

Diminished responsibility

If the defendant has been charged with murder, they can put forward a partial defence of diminished responsibility (Homicide Act 1957, s2). They are arguing that they have some culpability for the killing but not the full culpability required to be found guilty of murder. If the court agrees they will be found guilty of manslaughter rather than murder. If the defendant were to be convicted of murder, the judge would have no choice but to sentence them to life imprisonment, as a life sentence is mandatory in all cases where there is a murder conviction. The partial defence of diminished responsibility has been recently amended (Coroners and Justice Act 2009, s52). It requires that in order not to be convicted of murder, the defendant was suffering from abnormality of mental functioning which arose from a recognised medical condition and substantially impaired the defendant's ability to either understand the nature of their conduct, form a rational judgement or exercise self control, and that this provides an explanation for the defendant's acts or omissions in doing, or being a party to, the killing.

Once the accused has been found guilty of manslaughter by diminished responsibility they can be made subject to a range of sentences or disposals available to the court, from absolute discharge to life imprisonment. These disposals include the making of a hospital order with or without restrictions.

Hospital orders

Both the Magistrates' Court and the Crown Court can impose a hospital order (or a guardianship order) under section 37 of the Mental Health Act 1983 on convicting the offender. This is an alternative to prison, so the offence for which the offender has been found guilty needs to be one where a prison sentence can be imposed. There needs to be medical evidence that the grounds for a hospital order are met, from two doctors, one of whom is a specialist in mental disorder, and the grounds are similar to those required for admission under section 3 of the Act with the addition that the court is of the view that:

> having regard to all the circumstances including the nature of the offence and the character and antecedents of the offender, and to the other methods of dealing with him, that the most suitable method of disposing of the case is by means of an order under this section.

(MHA, s37(2)(b))

The grounds for a hospital order are dependent on the mental disorder present at the time of sentencing, not at the time of the offence or the trial. An offender can be mentally well at the time they committed the offence but still be sentenced to a hospital order because of the mental disorder that is present when they come to be sentenced by the court. In imposing a hospital order (or guardianship order) the court has decided not to punish the offender for the offence but send them to hospital instead. However, they have been convicted of the offence (unlike in cases of unfit to plead or a finding of not guilty by reason of insanity) and it will appear on the offender's criminal record. A hospital or guardianship order under this section cannot be imposed where the sentence is fixed by law, e.g. murder.

This order lasts for six months and can be extended for another six months and then yearly. For most practical purposes it runs like an admission under section 3, except the nearest relative does not have the power to discharge under section 23 and the patient cannot apply to the Mental Health Tribunal until after the first six months. The patient can be given medical treatment against their will.

If the offender has been convicted of a more serious offence and there are concerns about the risk to others, the Crown Court can impose a restriction order under section 41 at the same time as imposing a hospital order. This is called a hospital order with restrictions, or section 37/41. The grounds are the same for a hospital order but one of the two recommending doctors needs to give oral evidence in court. There is an additional requirement in that it appears to the court:

having regard to the nature of the offence, the antecedents of the offender and the risk of his committing further offences if set at large, that is necessary for the protection of the public from serious harm.

(MHA 1983, s41(1))

A restriction order is of indefinite duration, and is the equivalent in mental health law to a life sentence in penal law (Bartlett and Sandland, 2014: p370). The nature of the restriction order is that it brings the treatment of the patient under the supervision of the Ministry of Justice's (MoJ) Mental Health Casework Section (MHCS). The restrictions are imposed on the clinician in charge of the patient's treatment (the responsible clinician), which means they cannot grant leave, transfer to another hospital or discharge the patient without permission from the MoJ.

Restricted patients do not have nearest relatives within the meaning of the MHA. Other Part III patients have nearest relatives, but they do not have the power to discharge the patient. Both the Secretary of State for Justice and the Mental Health Tribunal have the power to discharge the patient either conditionally or absolutely. If the patient is conditionally discharged then they are subject to compulsory supervision and can be recalled back to hospital if they need further in-patient treatment. We will consider this in more detail later in the chapter.

Section 38 provides for the courts to impose an interim hospital order where they think a full hospital order might be appropriate. The offender has to be convicted of an offence punishable by imprisonment. Again the grounds are similar to a section 3, but with the addition that the court considers that it might be appropriate to impose a hospital order. It lasts for 12 weeks and then can be extended by the court for 28 days at a time to a maximum of one year. This order is primarily used to see if the offender is going to respond to treatment in hospital.

Hybrid order

As we have seen, when it comes to sentencing an offender for an offence, the courts have had a choice between either punishing the offender or diverting them into the mental health system by imposing a hospital order. Section 45A of the Mental Health Act 1983 allows the courts to do both at the same time by means of a hospital and limitation direction (known as a hybrid order). It allows the Crown Court, at the same time as imposing a prison sentence, to direct that the offender be immediately sent to hospital via a hospital direction with restrictions (similar to a section 41 restriction order). This is not available when the offender has been convicted of murder. The grounds are similar to those for a hospital order with restrictions. Treatment can be provided against the patient's wishes as with hospital orders.

The effect of a hybrid order is that the prison sentence and detention in hospital run alongside each other. If the hospital treatment is completed before the date the offender would be released from prison, then they can be transferred to prison. If they still need treatment in hospital the offender can remain in hospital beyond their prison release date. For indeterminate sentenced prisoners (e.g. life sentences) things are a little more complicated, as the parole board will be involved. Indeterminate sentenced prisoners do not have a release date but a tariff that must be served before they can be considered for release. Once this tariff expires they can be released, but only after the parole board decide that they no longer present a risk to the public. Indeterminate sentenced prisoners can stay in prison far longer than their original tariff if they still present a risk to the public on release.

Some have argued that the hybrid order undermines the principle of the diversion of mentally disordered offenders into treatment because it allows for the offender to be both punished and compelled into treatment at the same time. Bartlett and Sandland (2014: p396) argue that this reflects society's desire to punish rather than treat. It also illustrates the focus in public policy on protecting the public from the risk posed by the mentally disordered rather than the provision of high quality mental health services which could prevent the offending in the first place.

CASE STUDY

Matt

Matt is a 21-year-old White British man who does not have a formal mental disorder diagnosis. He has been under the care of the learning disability team since he turned 18, having being supported by children's services prior to that. He has recently been transferred to the community mental health team (CMHT) as it was found he did not have a learning disability. However, his problems are not typical of those who receive support from the CMHT either. Matt has at times come into contact with the police, in relation to allegations of offences involving dishonesty. His alleged offences usually have a strange and bizarre quality but are not the most serious. However, his behaviour is becoming more difficult to manage and attempts to divert him from the criminal justice system with increased support and social work interventions do not appear to be working. He is arrested in relation to an allegation of fraud which involved him saying that he had an expanding business and trying to obtain a large number of computers for this business.

He was examined by the FME and found fit to be interviewed. You are asked to be his appropriate adult. Is it appropriate for you to act as such and what factors do you need to take into account?

He is charged with one count of fraud and bailed to appear in court. How can you support and advise Matt during the court process? What issues might arise for you and him during this time?

He is found guilty at trial and the court is considering a prison sentence. What alternative mental health disposals are available to the court and how could these be arranged?

Powers after sentence

There are situations where the offender's mental disorder does not become apparent until after they have been sentenced to a period of imprisonment, or the mental disorder at the time of sentence was not sufficient to divert the offender into treatment at that stage. In such cases the Secretary of State for Justice has the power to direct the transfer of a prisoner to hospital.

Power of the Secretary of State to transfer

Section 47 of the Mental Health Act 1983 gives the Secretary of State the power to direct the transfer of a sentenced prisoner to hospital. This is called a transfer direction. There needs to be the medical evidence (from two doctors) that transfer to hospital is required. These are similar to the grounds for a hospital order and the prisoner can be given treatment against their will. The prisoner can be transferred back to prison at any time before their prison sentence expires if they no longer need medical treatment in hospital.

Most of the time a section 47 transfer direction is accompanied by a restriction direction under section 49 (similar to a restriction order under section 41). These apply the same restrictions on discharge, transfer and leave as a restriction order. However, if the patient remains in hospital after the expiry of the prison sentence and they would have been released if they were still in prison, the restriction direction ends and they become an unrestricted patient. This is called a 'notional 37' to show that they are now effectively an unrestricted hospital order patient.

A prisoner can appeal to the Mental Health Tribunal on transfer and then yearly. However, if they still have a prison sentence left to run, this could result in them being transferred back to prison rather than being discharged from hospital. The provisions for indeterminate prisoners are more complicated (as their sentence does not expire in the same way) and they cannot be released direct from hospital without the permission of the Parole Board or the Secretary of State.

Powers on release from hospital and in the community

There are powers available to ensure that mentally disordered offenders receive treatment in the community (although they cannot be forced to have this treatment in the same way as in hospital) both following a period of hospital treatment and as an alternative to prison or hospital.

Mental health treatment requirement

The Criminal Justice Act 2003 allows for offenders to be sentenced to a community order (formerly called a probation order) instead of sending them to prison. When such an order is imposed the court can impose a range of requirements on the offender. These include drug rehabilitation, alcohol treatment and mental health treatment. The court must have decided the mental disorder is such that the offender requires treatment but that a guardianship order or hospital order under section 37 of the Mental Health Act is not appropriate. The court cannot impose such a requirement without the offender saying that they are willing to comply with it.

The offender is not detained under the MHA and cannot be forced to have treatment against their will.

Social supervision of conditionally discharged patients

As we have discussed, a patient detained under section 37/41 (hospital order with restrictions) can be discharged from hospital either absolutely or conditionally. An absolute discharge is the same as a discharge from section 2 or 3. The patient is free to go and does not have to comply with any treatment or supervision in the community if they do not want to. An absolute discharge from hospital is rare and is more likely to happen after a significant period of conditional discharge.

When a patient is conditionally discharged, the Secretary of State for Justice has the power to recall them to hospital if they need further treatment. When a patient is conditionally discharged they have to be allocated a clinical supervisor (a consultant psychiatrist) and a social supervisor (a social worker, occupational therapist or a nurse). The role of these supervisors is set out in Ministry of Justice guidance (MoJ, 2009) and is available electronically. If you are working in a mental health or learning disability team it is likely that you will be asked to be a social supervisor at some point in your career. This role should be reserved for experienced practitioners and preferably those who are approved mental health professionals. You could certainly not take on this role without undertaking specialist training and without supervision from someone who understands the role and its requirements.

A recent inquiry into the care and treatment of Peter Bryan (NHS London, 2009) was very critical of the lack of experience of both the clinical and social supervisors in this case. Peter Bryan killed a man while a conditionally discharged patient, after previously killing a woman. He quite quickly then went on to kill another patient whilst he was detained in Broadmoor Hospital. The social supervisor had not previously worked in mental health and while he was enthusiastic about his role, the inquiry found 'enthusiasm is no substitute for experience'. The inquiry stated:

> If any single lesson can be learned from the analysis of the care of PB, it should be that responsibility for managing and treating s37/41 patients should only be given to professionals who have sufficient experience and training to look after such individuals . . . There was . . . a systemic failure to ensure that the key professionals allocated to care for PB in the community had the experience necessary to deal with someone with his forensic history and complex presentation.

The inquiry recommended that the MoJ should issue guidance to state that social supervisors should be what are now called approved mental health professionals and have at least two years' experience as AMHPs. The Ministry of Justice has not, as yet, implemented this condition.

The MoJ guidance on the role of a social supervisor sets out expectations, including home visiting, reports to the MoJ, sharing information, ongoing risk assessment, working with the clinical supervisor and having a view on recall. If you are working as a social supervisor, it is worth getting to know how the Mental Health Casework

Section in the Ministry of Justice operates. Cases are allocated according to the surname of the patient so it is possible to find out which officer is dealing with your patient and make contact with them over and above the quarterly reports that you are required to send. You will find a contact list on the Ministry of Justice website.

The recall of a conditionally discharged patient is a last resort and should only be done when they need to be in hospital because of deteriorating mental health or there is an increased risk due to their mental state. It needs to be based on up-to-date medical evidence (*Kay v UK* 17821/91 [1994] ECHR 51). The Ministry of Justice makes the decision to recall based on the information provided by the clinical and social supervisors and then issues a warrant of recall. The supervisors have to then find a bed and make the arrangements for the patient to be admitted. Once a patient is recalled the Secretary of State for Justice has to refer them to the Mental Health Tribunal.

Multi-agency public protection arrangements (MAPPA)

Working with mentally disordered offenders in the community can be challenging and demanding work, especially if they have the potential to present as a significant risk to others. This work will involve collaborating with other agencies. The framework for this in the case of higher risk offenders is the multi-agency public protection arrangements (MAPPA). These arrangements are in place to ensure that violent and sexual offenders are properly managed. You will have a MAPPA panel that meets regularly in your area and you should be familiar with how it works and who from your agency attends. Guidance on MAPPA can be found from the Ministry of Justice (2014) and there should be local training available for agencies who have a duty to cooperate with MAPPA.

CHAPTER SUMMARY

- Government policy with regard to mentally disordered offenders rests on three basic principles: they need special safeguards when in custody; they should be diverted away from the criminal justice system where possible; and (controversially) the public requires protection against the risk posed by mentally disordered people.

- Before the police can interview a detainee, the custody officer has to be sure that they are fit to be interviewed.

- People who might be mentally vulnerable need an appropriate adult to be present when they are being interviewed by the police.

- There is a range of provisions within Part III of the Mental Health Act with regard to mentally disordered offenders.

- Restricted hospital order patients can be conditionally discharged from hospital and made subject to supervision. These patients can be recalled to hospital by the Ministry of Justice if they need further in-patient treatment.

Bradley, K (2009) *The Bradley Report: Lord Bradley's Review of People with Mental Health Problems or Learning Disabilities in the Criminal Justice System.* London: Department of Health.

Lord Bradley's report on what changes are needed to the provision of care to mentally disordered offenders.

Department of Health (2015) *Mental Health Act 1983: Code of Practice.* London: TSO.

Chapter 22 gives guidance with regard to patients concerned with criminal proceedings.

Chapter 9

Deprivation of Liberty Safeguards

ACHIEVING A SOCIAL WORK DEGREE

This chapter will help you to develop the following capabilities from the Professional Capabilities Framework:

- **Professionalism**
  Identify and behave as a professional social worker committed to professional development.

- **Values and ethics**
  Apply social work ethical principles and values to guide professional practice.

- **Rights, justice and economic well-being**
  Advance human rights and promote social justice and economic well-being.

- **Knowledge**
  Apply the knowledge of social sciences, law and social work practice theory.

- **Intervention and skills**
  Use judgement and authority to intervene with individuals, families and communities to promote independence, provide support and prevent harm, neglect and abuse.

It will also help you develop the following National Occupational Standards for Social Work in Wales:

- **Maintain professional accountability**
  SW 1: Maintain an up-to-date knowledge and evidence base for social work practice.

- **Practise professional social work**
  SW 4: Exercise professional judgement in social work.

- **Promote engagement and participation**
  SW 9: Engage people in social work practice.
  SW 10: Support people to participate in decision-making processes.
  SW 11: Advocate on behalf of people.

Introduction

The Deprivation of Liberty Safeguards (DOLS) have been in force since April 2009 and have been controversial from the beginning. The criticisms have focused on the complexity of the safeguards and the difficulties in understanding what is (and is not) a deprivation of liberty. As a result, social workers may be tempted to avoid this subject altogether and leave it to the experts. These provisions are exactly what they say they are, safeguards, and you need to know when they need to be applied in working with adults who lack the capacity to make the decisions around their care or medical treatment. If you are not a qualified assessor under Deprivation of Liberty safeguards, you will not be required to make the decision that a person is being deprived of their liberty. However, you may be involved in placing people into residential care, hospital or supported living (or reviewing such placements) and as such you need to understand what is, and what is not, a deprivation of liberty. If you do not have this understanding, you may inadvertently place a person into conditions that amount to a deprivation of liberty without lawful authority.

This chapter aims to provide an introduction to the Deprivation of Liberty Safeguards. We will explore how these safeguards came about and to whom they apply. We will then go on to explore the difference between restrictions on liberty and deprivation of liberty so that you can be confident in understanding when the safeguards should be applied. The safeguards themselves will be examined so that you have a basic understanding of the process and the professionals involved. The chapter will conclude by discussing when DOLS cannot be used and what needs to happen instead.

The Deprivation of Liberty Safeguards is an amendment to the Mental Capacity Act 2005 in the form of schedules A1 and 1A. These amendments were introduced by means of the Mental Health Act 2007. At the same time the Government introduced a supplement to the Mental Capacity Act Code of Practice (Department of Constitutional Affairs, 2007), which we shall refer to as the Deprivation of Liberty Code of Practice (DOLS Code) (Ministry of Justice, 2008). The DOLS Code is easy to read and short (120 pages) so it is a recommended read if you want to understand the safeguards in more detail. DOLS is designed to prevent a person, who lacks the capacity to make decisions about their treatment and care in a care home or hospital, being deprived of their liberty without lawful authority. In other words, it is designed to prevent breaches of Article 5 of the European Convention on Human Rights (ECHR), the right to liberty. We explored this Convention right in Chapter 3 and the fact that the Mental Health Act 1983 provides a procedure prescribed by law by which people who have an 'unsound mind' can be deprived of their liberty in order to provide treatment for their mental disorder. DOLS provides another procedure prescribed by law, in which people who do not have the capacity to make decisions about their treatment or care can be deprived of their liberty so that treatment or care can be provided. As we will see, DOLS was designed to fill a gap in the law that was not covered by the Mental Health Act 1983.

Why do we have DOLS?

DOLS was introduced after the UK Government lost a case in the European Court of Human Rights. This case has now become a very well-known case called *HL v UK* (2004 40 EHHR 761) and any consideration of DOLS would not be complete without considering this case. Before this case there was no formal legal process which covered people who lacked capacity being admitted to care homes or hospitals (Bartlett and Sandland, 2014: p203). There was the common law doctrine of 'necessity' which has now mostly been superseded by the Mental Capacity Act 2005. However, prior to the DOLS amendments, the MCA could not be used to deprive a person of liberty.

The case of HL concerns a 48-year-old man with autism who was admitted informally to Bournewood Hospital in Surrey, a psychiatric hospital, in 1997. He had had autism since birth, was unable to speak, his ability to understand the world around him was limited, and he was frequently agitated and resorted to self-harm. He spent 30 years being cared for in Bournewood Hospital, but in 1994 he was discharged into the care of adult carers (DOLS Code, para 2.22). During a routine visit to a day centre HL became agitated and his behaviour became unmanageable; he started hitting his head and banging his head against the wall. The day centre staff could not get hold of his carers so he was sedated, taken to Accident and Emergency and then admitted to Bournewood Hospital as an informal patient (Barber et al., 2012: p80). As he did not resist his admission, it was considered that it was not necessary to detain him under the MHA. However, his carers were not happy about this readmission and requested to have HL released into their care. The staff at the hospital refused, and the carers were not able to visit him in hospital for at least three months. The case was taken to court and eventually ended up in the European Court of Human Rights who found that HL had been deprived of his liberty unlawfully. As there was no procedure prescribed by law that could authorise the deprivation of liberty in HL's case, the Government introduced the Deprivation of Liberty Safeguards. The MHA was not used in HL's case because he complied with (or at least did not resist) his admission. However, he was nevertheless deprived of his liberty and this cannot be lawful unless the provisions of Article 5 ECHR are complied with.

It is useful to consider the restrictions that were being placed on HL as this can help to understand what factors need to be taken into account when considering if a deprivation of liberty exists. Barber et al. (2012: p81) state that the restrictions included:

- administration of sedative medication both before and after admission to hospital
- admission to an in-patient unit
- no contact with his carers
- requests by his carers for HL to be discharged into their care refused
- he was not free to leave the hospital
- he was under continuous supervision by hospital staff
- he was given treatment without his consent

The European Court found that he was deprived of his liberty because he 'was under continuous supervision and not free to leave' (Jones, 2012: 2–002). The court considered that it was the 'degree and intensity' of all these restrictions which amounted to a deprivation of liberty in the case of HL (Barber et al., 2012: p81).

However, when they introduced DOLS, the Government decided not to provide a statutory definition of a deprivation of liberty. Instead it stated that references to deprivation of liberty have the same meaning as Article 5(1) of the European Convention on Human Rights (MCA 2005, s64(5)). This means that there is no clear statutory definition (defined by Parliament in legislation) of what is a deprivation of liberty. Instead, it is up to the courts to interpret what the Convention means by deprivation of liberty, which means that what is considered to be deprivation of liberty can change over time.

Restrictions on liberty and deprivation of liberty

In order to understand if a person is likely to a deprived of their liberty, you need to understand what restrictions on their liberty are being imposed. As with deprivation of liberty, there is no definition of restrictions on liberty. There have been a number of cases since the introduction of DOLS which have placed differing emphasis on a range of restrictions in order to decide whether there is a deprivation of liberty or not. However, what is clear is that a deprivation of liberty occurs when the 'intensity and degree' of the restrictions placed on the person, who lacks capacity and is in a care home or hospital, build up to a point where the threshold of deprivation of liberty is crossed. Now this threshold of deprivation of liberty has changed over time (and is likely to continue to change in the absence of a statutory definition) but the fundamental building blocks, i.e. restrictions on liberty, basically remain the same. If we continue with the analogy of building blocks, restrictions can be bigger or smaller but when they are built on top of each other they can be tall enough to show that the threshold required for deprivation of liberty has been reached. This can be made up of a larger number of smaller blocks, or a smaller number of bigger blocks, or more often a combination of various sized blocks. If when you add up all the restrictions, the threshold of deprivation of liberty has not been reached, then there is no need for a legal authorisation.

How do you identify restrictions on liberty? The DOLS Code gives some guidance on what are restrictions on liberty. However, they must be considered in the light of case law, as things have moved on since the Code was written. Nevertheless, the Code (para 2.5) does provide a reasonable starting point in considering the restrictions in place:

- Restraint is used, including sedation, to admit a person to an institution where that person is resisting admission.
- Staff exercise complete and effective control over the care and movement of a person for a significant period.
- Staff exercise control over assessments, treatment, contacts and residence.
- A decision has been taken by the institution that the person will not be released into the care of others, or permitted to live elsewhere, unless the staff in the institution consider it appropriate.
- A request by carers for a person to be discharged to their care is refused.
- The person is unable to maintain social contacts because of restrictions placed on their access to other people.
- The person loses autonomy because they are under continuous supervision and control.

This is by no means an exhaustive list of what restrictions could apply in a care home or in hospital. It is important to consider factors that might apply to most people in care homes or hospital but are still restrictions on liberty, such as restricted visiting times, routines, fixed meal times, limited food choices, provision of personal care, medication used to manage behaviour, only being allowed out with an escort, not being allowed to visit certain places and restriction on visitors. These factors alone may not amount to a deprivation of liberty but overall the 'intensity and degree' of these restrictions may do so.

ACTIVITY 9.1

Identifying restrictions on liberty

Think about a situation where you visited or worked with a person in residential care. What restrictions were being placed on the person? Try and think about the less obvious and seemingly innocuous ones because they can all add up to have a significant impact on the person.

Once the restrictions on liberty have been identified, and from the exercise above we can see that this is not always straightforward, how is it decided that they amount to a deprivation of liberty? As we have already stated, there have been numerous court cases which have resulted in the threshold for a finding of deprivation of liberty changing over time. However, there are three conditions that must be satisfied before there can be a deprivation of liberty (*Storck v Germany* (61603/00) [2005] 1 MHLR 211):

- **Objective element** – a person's confinement in a certain limited place for a not negligible period of time.

- **Subjective element** – the person has not (or has not been able to) validly consented to the confinement in question.

- **Responsibility of the state** – the deprivation of liberty must be one for which the state is responsible.

There has been considerable debate about when considering the objective element, where the correct threshold is for finding that a person's confinement amounts to a deprivation of liberty. In March 2014, the UK Supreme Court considered this issue for the first time in a case that has been become known as the 'Cheshire West' case (*P v Cheshire West and Chester Council and another; P and Q v Surrey County Council* [2014] UKSC 19). This judgment was long awaited and has clarified the meaning of deprivation of liberty. It has effectively reduced the threshold for a finding of deprivation of liberty. As a result, many more people have come within the DOLS provisions, and local authorities have been swamped with requests by care homes and hospitals for DOLS assessments (Community Care, 2014).

Lady Hale gave the lead judgment in the Cheshire West case and provides, following a detailed evaluation of the case law on deprivation of liberty to date, an apparently straightforward definition of what is a deprivation of liberty in cases where the person is not able to consent. That is: the person is not free to leave, and is under continuous supervision and control. This has been described as the 'acid test' as to whether or not a person is deprived of their liberty. The court also set out factors that are not relevant to an assessment of deprivation of liberty. These are: whether or not the person is objecting to their living arrangements, the relative normality of the placement, and the reason or purpose behind the placement in the care home or hospital. If the person is acquiescing and not resisting or objecting to the restrictions, it still could be that they are being deprived of their liberty. Even if the care home or hospital is trying to act in the best interests of the person, and the purpose behind the restrictions is benevolent, there could still be a deprivation of liberty. Restrictions imposed for good and kind reasons can still cause a deprivation of liberty and as such it still needs to be authorised. The 'relative normality' factor comes from a previous court judgment which considered how close to a normal environment of a family home the placement is.

Lady Hale in this judgment went on to criticise the Deprivation of Liberty Safeguards themselves:

> The safeguards have the appearance of bewildering complexity, much greater than the comparable provisions for detaining mental patients in hospital under the Mental Health Act.

(para 9)

This followed the criticism of DOLS by the House of Lords (2014) which found that DOLS was not fit for purpose and that:

> the Government needs to go back to the drawing board to draft replacement provisions that are easy to understand and implement, and in keeping with the style and ethos of the MCA.

To date the Government has no plans to replace DOLS but has asked the Law Commission to undertake a review (Law Commission, 2014).

As we have seen the new 'acid test' of deprivation of liberty is threefold:

- Is the person free to leave?
- Is the person subject to continuous supervision?
- Does that supervision amount to continuous supervision *and* control?

It is tempting to think that this reduced threshold means that most people in care homes and long-term hospital care will be deprived of their liberty, and this concern may be behind most of the increase in referrals for DOLS assessments. However, it is not clear that this was the intention of the Supreme Court and, as we shall see, it is still a test that needs to be rigorously applied to each individual case.

Free to leave

This is more than just not being able (or allowed) to leave the care home or hospital to visit friends, go to the shops or meet with friends in the pub. While this could be considered as being not free to leave, in most cases the care home or hospital could facilitate such visits and trips out with support from staff or relatives. A person could be free to leave to go out on visits, with support or supervision, if required, but they may not be free to leave and go and live elsewhere if they so wished.

Remember we are talking about people who do not have the capacity to make decisions about their living arrangements, so any expressed wish may not be a capacious decision. However, the attitude of the public authority that arranged the placement is key here. If the person, or their relatives, expressed a wish for them to move into another placement or other living arrangement, what would the authority's approach be? If the approach is to consider the request at the time in the light of the current circumstances with an open mind in considering what is in the person's best interests, then the person may be free to leave. The reality is that most people placed in care homes funded by public authorities would not be free to leave without the providers and commissioners of their care deciding that this would be in their best interests. If the approach is that if the person wanted to live elsewhere and the authorities have made the decision that would not be possible, then the person is not free to leave. However, just because a person is not free to leave does not mean that they are deprived of their liberty.

Continuous supervision and control

What amounts to continuous supervision and control was not discussed in Lady Hale's judgment but this does follow from previous cases including the HL case we discussed earlier. The factors in this case continue to be relevant in deciding whether or not a person is subject to continuous supervision and control. It is important to note that continuous supervision on its own is not enough for a deprivation of liberty; there has to be continuous supervision *and* control. Some have argued that most people in care homes or hospitals are subject to continuous supervision. It is true that most people would be subject to periodic or frequent supervision but does this amount to continuous supervision? If a person has a member of staff watching them all the time, day and night, then it is difficult to argue that this is not continuous supervision. But, what about hourly checks, or checks every 15 minutes or every five minutes? Ultimately, whether this amounts to a deprivation of liberty or not is down to the professional undertaking this assessment under DOLS, and they would have to take into account a broader range of factors rather than just the frequency of supervision. In order for there to be a deprivation of liberty the supervision has to also amount to control. If the continuous supervision is in place to enable staff to quickly restrain them if they try to harm themselves, to stop them absconding, to prevent them running into traffic when they are outside, then it could be argued that this is supervision and control. Remember the supervision and control have to be continuous, or effectively continuous, before they could be considered to lead to a deprivation of liberty.

Unless you have been trained to be an assessor under Deprivation of Liberty Safeguards, you will not be required to make the decision that a person is being deprived of their liberty in a care home or hospital. However, if you are making arrangements for a person to be moved into a care home or hospital, having assessed their capacity, found they lack it, and made the decision that it is in their best interests, you do need to decide if it is likely, or not, that the care they need in the home or hospital can only be provided in conditions that amount to a deprivation of liberty. If you feel that it is likely that the person will be deprived of their liberty, considering all the factors we have discussed, then it will be your duty to ensure that the DOLS processes are followed and that any deprivation of liberty is lawfully authorised (DOLS Code, paras 9.1–9.7).

ACTIVITY **9.2**

When might a deprivation of liberty be occurring?

Imagine a case where you are making arrangements for a person to be transferred to a residential care setting from a hospital after a fall. The person does not have the capacity to consent to being accommodated in a care home. Think about what restrictions might apply to this person in the home. Now think about what would need to be happening to the person in order for you to think that a deprivation of liberty might be occurring. What factors do you have to take into account in such situations?

The standard authorisation

When a person who lacks the capacity to make decisions about their treatment or care is being, or is likely to be, deprived of their liberty in a hospital or care home, the DOLS procedures should be triggered. It is the 'managing authority' that is responsible for applying for the authorisation to deprive the person of their liberty (called a standard authorisation). Paragraph 3.1 of the DOLS Code states that the managing authority of a care home or independent hospital is the person who is the registered manager of that home or hospital under the Care Standards Act 2000. In the case of an NHS hospital, it is the NHS body that is responsible for the running of that hospital.

If you think that an authorisation is needed, because the person is being or likely to be deprived of their liberty, then you must inform the managing authority of the hospital or home in which the person is placed (or is going to be placed) (DOLS Code, para 3.2). If the hospital or care home do not agree with you or do not understand their responsibilities under DOLS and do not make an application for a standard authorisation, then you might need to consider using your local authority's adult safeguarding procedures because the person may be unlawfully deprived of their liberty.

Applications for a standard authorisation can be made up to 28 days in advance, so if you are placing a person in a care home or hospital, it is possible for the arrangements to be made to authorise the deprivation of liberty before the person arrives (DOLS Code, 3.5). The 'supervisory body' is responsible for considering requests for authorisations, commissioning the required assessments and authorising the deprivation of liberty. Following the implementation of the Health and Social Care Act 2012, the supervisory body is now the local authority for the area in which the person is ordinarily resident. The test of ordinary residence has been updated with the implementation of the Care Act 2014 (s39) and its associated regulations. In most cases it will be the local authority that are funding the placement in the care home, even if the care home is outside the area of the funding local authority. If the person is self-funding then they will usually be ordinarily resident in the local authority area in which the care home is located. The same principles also apply to a person in NHS accommodation.

Once the supervisory body (SB) receives the application from the managing authority (MA) for a standard authorisation (the DOLS Code, paras 3.7–3.9, sets out what information should be provided) then the SB has 21 days from when they received the application to complete the required assessments, make the decision and issue the standard authorisation. However, if the case is urgent (i.e. it is likely that the person is already being deprived of their liberty) then the MA can give themselves an urgent authorisation at the same time as making the application for a standard authorisation. In such cases, the SB has to complete the assessments within seven days of the urgent authorisation being given. The urgent authorisation can be extended by seven days in exceptional circumstances.

Once the SB decides to proceed with the application it has to commission the six assessments required under DOLS. There are two different assessors who are required to undertake these assessments: the mental health assessor (MH) and the best interests assessor (BIA). The mental health assessor is a doctor with experience in the treatment and diagnosis of mental disorders who has undertaken training to become a DOLS assessor. A BIA has to be a social worker, nurse, occupational therapist or psychologist. All need to be two years post qualification and to have undertaken training to be a BIA.

Age

The person must be, or believed to be, 18 years or older at the point that the standard authorisation would come into force. This assessment is undertaken by the BIA.

No refusals

This is undertaken by the BIA who has to establish if the deprivation of liberty would conflict with another form of decision making for the person. This would include an advance decision made by the person, the decision of a donee of a relevant Lasting Power of Attorney (LPA) by the person, or a decision of a deputy appointed by the Court of Protection (LPA and the Court of Protection will be discussed in Chapter 10).

Mental capacity

This assessment can be undertaken by the BIA or the MH assessor. The assessor is required to assess capacity in relation to the decision to be accommodated in the care home or hospital for the purpose of receiving care or treatment. Capacity assessments have been discussed in Chapter 4 and the same process has to be followed here.

Mental health

This assessment can only be undertaken by an MH assessor. The doctor has to determine if the person has a mental disorder within the meaning of the Mental Health Act 1983. This was discussed in Chapter 3. The learning disability qualification for longer-term sections under the Mental Health Act does not apply to DOLS, i.e. the learning disability does not have to be associated with abnormally aggressive or seriously irresponsible conduct in order for DOLS to apply. As a result DOLS could be used for people with a learning disability in situations where the MHA could not be applied.

Eligibility

This assessment can be undertaken by the MH assessor or a BIA who is also an AMHP. This is not an easy assessment to understand, as the requirements are different for a person in a care home or a hospital. If the person is in a care home, the assessor has to simply determine that they are not currently detained in hospital under the MHA. They can be subject to DOLS if they are on section 17 from hospital, on a guardianship order, subject to conditional discharge as a restricted patient, or on a community treatment order as long as the standard authorisation does not conflict with the requirements placed on the person under the MHA. If the person is being deprived of their liberty in hospital for treatment for a mental disorder, the situation is more complicated. It is expected that in such cases the MHA would be used, but there are certain situations where the MHA cannot be used (such as some learning disability cases) or there is a choice between MHA and DOLS (if the patient is not objecting to their treatment or care in hospital).

Best interests

This is undertaken by a BIA and they have to address four questions:

- Is the person's treatment and care in a care home or hospital amounting to, or will it amount to, a deprivation of liberty?
- Is it in the best interests of the person to be deprived of their liberty?
- Is it necessary to deprive the person of their liberty to prevent them coming to harm?
- Is the deprivation of liberty proportionate to the likelihood that they would come to harm and the seriousness of the harm if it were to occur?

We have discussed the deprivation of liberty element of this assessment. The best interests element is much the same as the best interests requirements under section 4 of the Mental Capacity Act. The BIA has to consider if there are less restrictive ways of providing the care and treatment and if a deprivation of liberty could be avoided. A BIA could decide that the person was being deprived of their liberty but it was not in their best interests, as there was a less restrictive alternative such as reducing the restrictions so they did not amount to continuous supervision and control, or that the person should be free to leave and return to independent accommodation. Only harm to the person themselves can be considered as part of this assessment, as the MCA cannot be used to solely prevent the person causing harm to other people.

Chapter 4 of the DOLS Code sets out these assessments in more detail. If the person fails any one of these assessments then a standard authorisation cannot be given. If the person has capacity to make decisions regarding their treatment and care, then only the care and treatment to which they consent can be given, and if they want to return home or independent accommodation then this needs to be arranged. If they are not deprived of their liberty then an authorisation is not required. If they are deprived of their liberty and it is not in their best interests, then the deprivation of liberty must end by either the restrictions being reduced to below the threshold or the person moved into conditions which do not amount to deprivation of liberty. We can see that the BIA has a powerful role here to ensure that both any unnecessary deprivations of liberty are avoided and that any care provided to an incapacitated person in a care home or hospital is always in the person's best interests.

If all of these assessments are passed then the SB has to issue a standard authorisation. The length of the standard authorisation can be for up to one year but it cannot be longer than the period recommended by the BIA in the best interests assessment. Conditions on the managing authority can be added to the standard authorisation with the purpose of either preventing the need for a deprivation of liberty in the future or ensuring that the deprivation of liberty is in the person's best interests. The SB also has to appoint a person to be the relevant person's representative (RPR). This role provides some important safeguards and is discussed in Chapter 10.

When an application under the MHA is made and the patient is admitted they are deprived of their liberty by virtue of the completed application paperwork. The restrictions placed on the patient whilst they are in hospital are not relevant to the issue of deprivation of liberty. They are deprived of liberty because of their legal status. With regard to the DOLS standard authorisation, the situation is very different. The standard authorisation does not cause the person to be deprived of their liberty, as it is the restrictions in place in the care home or hospital that do that. All the standard authorisation does is permit the care home or hospital to deprive the person of their liberty but it does not require them to do this (DOLS Code, para 8.8). Therefore, the care home or hospital could remove the deprivation of liberty at any time by simply reducing the restrictions to below the threshold and applying to the SB for a review. As a result, it is important that the restrictions are reviewed periodically to ensure that a person is not deprived of their liberty for any longer than is in their best interests.

The following case study illustrates how the Deprivation of Liberty Safeguards might work in practice.

CASE STUDY

Jacob

Jacob is a Black British man in his 80s who is in a care home. He has a diagnosis of Lewy body dementia and experiences a wide range of symptoms. Until recently these have been well managed at the care home where he has lived for a number of years. However, he has now become resistant to his care. He keeps talking about wanting to go home, though he has previously expressed satisfaction with being in the care home. He now needs restraining on a frequent basis to stop him taking other residents' food and belongings. Whilst

(Continued)

141

this restraint is minimal in terms of duration, its use is becoming more frequent and he is much more closely monitored. He now needs more support with his self-care. However, his son has been happy with the care provided to his father and he wishes for him to stay at this care home. The manager of the home is concerned that Jacob is being deprived of his liberty by the actions of the staff providing the care and she does not think that Jacob has the mental capacity to consent to these arrangements. She makes a referral to the local authority that is funding Jacob's care for a standard authorisation under DOLS, and gives the home an urgent authorisation as she feels that Jacob is currently deprived of his liberty.

The local authority (the supervisory body) arranges for a mental health assessor and a best interests assessor (BIA) to assess Jacob. The mental health assessor agrees that Jacob has a mental disorder, namely dementia, that he lacks the capacity to make decisions about being accommodated in a care home and receiving care, and that he is eligible for a standard authorisation because he is not subject to any provisions of the Mental Health Act 1983.

The BIA finds that Jacob's son has a Lasting Power of Attorney for both finance and welfare decisions but he does not object to his father being in the care home under the current restrictions. The BIA, after considering the views of the son, the staff at the home and those of the care manager at the local authority, finds that Jacob is deprived of his liberty because he is not free to leave and subject to continuous supervision and control. She decides that the deprivation of his liberty is in his best interests because he has been at the home for many years, they know him well and are still able to meet his needs. Without the increased level of supervision and control, he would not be able to stay in the home and given how content he was there until recently, she feels that he would want to stay there. His son is able to visit several times a week and speaks highly of the staff and the care that his father receives. They are still managing to support Jacob with visits to a local church and club that he has been attending for many years.

The BIA makes a recommendation that the home arranges for an occupational therapy assessment to see if there is a less restrictive way of managing his behaviour and a standard authorisation is given for six months in the first instance. His son is appointed as Jacob's relevant person's representative (RPR).

When DOLS cannot be used to authorise a deprivation of liberty

There are certain situations when the Deprivation of Liberty Safeguards cannot be used to authorise a deprivation of liberty.

We have already noted that DOLS only applies in registered care homes or hospitals. It cannot be used where the person is, or is going to be, accommodated in a supported living arrangement. These arrangements usually involve the person having a tenancy agreement with support provided by paid staff. If a person lacks the capacity to make decisions regarding being accommodated in a supported living arrangement, then there may be an issue as to whether they have the capacity to enter into a contract such as a tenancy agreement. The issue of incapacity and tenancy agreements has been considered by the courts and the Court of Protection has issued guidance on the issue (Court of Protection, 2012). The important issue here is that the MCA cannot be used to authorise someone signing a tenancy on another person's behalf, even if it is in the person's best interests, unless they are authorised by a Lasting Power of Attorney, deputyship from the Court of Protection or by an order from the Court of Protection. If the restrictions under which an incapacitated person is accommodated in a supported living arrangement are likely to amount to a deprivation of liberty, this can only be authorised by an application to the Court of Protection. The Law Commission are examining this issue as part of their review of DOLS.

DOLS also cannot be used as a means by which public authorities can exercise their will against the wishes of relatives of the person. This point arose out of a high profile case in which the local authority was found to have acted unlawfully in firstly depriving a person of their liberty without legal authority and later by using DOLS to prevent the person returning home to live with his father. This case is unusual in that the person who was the subject of the proceedings was named: Steven Neary (*LB Hillingdon v Steven Neary and others* [2011] EWHC 1377 (COP)). Mark Neary, Steven's father, has written an account of events leading up to the court case, which is worth a read (Neary, 2011).

Steven has childhood autism and a severe learning disability. He requires support and supervision at all times. His behaviour at times can be very challenging, usually when his normal routine is disturbed. He lived with his father with high levels of support from the London Borough of Hillingdon social services department. In December 2009 Steven went into respite care earlier than planned at the request of his father due to his father being unwell. It was then arranged for Steven to be moved into a support unit for a 'couple of weeks' to give his father a chance to recover, again with his father's agreement. However, at the end of the two weeks, Steven was not allowed home despite his father's insistence that he should be. He remained at the unit under restrictions that the court found amounted to a deprivation of liberty but without any authorisation until April 2010 when Steven was made subject to a DOLS standard authorisation. He was then subject to three standard authorisations between April 2010 and the end of that year.

The court found that Steven had been deprived of his liberty between January and April 2010 and because there was no standard authorisation in place, this was unlawful. The also court found that the standard authorisations used after April were unlawful because of weaknesses in the DOLS assessments of what was in Steven's best interests. The court also found that Hillingdon had acted unlawfully by not appointing an IMCA until November 2010 and not conducting a review of the best interests requirements. The court criticised Hillingdon for the poor quality decision making and the negative attitude its staff had towards Mark Neary, which resulted in them not acting in Steven's best interests.

In his judgment Jackson J stated (para 22):

> The ordinary powers of a local authority are limited to investigating, providing support services, and where appropriate referring the matter to the court. If a local authority

seeks to regulate, control, compel, restrain, confine or coerce it must, except in an emergency, point to specific statutory authority for what it is doing or else obtain the appropriate sanction of the court.

The judge found that the DOLS standard authorisations were not lawful because they did not properly consider Steven's best interests and less restrictive options, i.e. him returning home to live with his father. As a result of this judgment, if a supervisory body is considering depriving a person of their liberty in the face of objections by relatives, it should try and resolve these disagreements, and if it cannot then the matter needs to be referred to the Court of Protection.

As a result of the court's decision, Steven returned home to live with his father and at the time of writing he still lives independently with support from paid carers and his father.

CHAPTER SUMMARY

- The Deprivation of Liberty Safeguards were introduced to provide a legal process by which people who lack capacity to make decisions regarding their care in a hospital or care home can have their deprivation of liberty authorised.

- The acid test of deprivation of liberty is that a person is subject to restrictions in a care home or hospital which mean that the person is not free to leave and is subject to continuous supervision and control.

- The care home or hospital has to apply to the local authority for a standard authorisation.

- There are six assessments that need to be carried out and these are done by two professionals: a mental health assessor and a best interests assessor.

- DOLS cannot be used in supported living environments or in a person's own home. Also, DOLS cannot be used to overcome objections by a person's relatives. In these cases, a local authority needs to make an application to the Court of Protection to authorise the deprivation of liberty.

FURTHER READING

Brown, R, Barber P and Martin, D (2009) *The Mental Capacity Act 2005: A Guide for Practice*, 2nd edition. Exeter: Learning Matters.

Chapter 16 discusses the Deprivation of Liberty Safeguards in more detail.

Neary, M (2011) *Get Steven Home*. Lulu.com

Mark Neary talking about what happened to his son Steven when the Deprivation of Liberty Safeguards were not lawfully applied.

Chapter 10
Safeguards

Introduction

Throughout this book we have discussed the significant powers that the Mental Health Act 1983 (MHA) and the Mental Capacity Act 2005 (MCA) give to professionals to make decisions on behalf of those who are not able to make decisions because of a mental disorder or because they lack the capacity to do so. Such decisions can result in people being deprived of their liberty for an indefinite period, or at the very least, significant restrictions being imposed to which they have not consented. In most cases, those working on behalf of public authorities do not have to apply to the courts to exercise these powers. Both Acts have significant safeguards to balance the powers invested in public bodies. In this chapter we will explore these safeguards so that you as social workers will be able to support those with whom you are working in exercising these safeguards if they so wish. Safeguards are no safeguards at all if people cannot access them. They cannot access them if they do not know about them and in some cases if they are not supported to access them.

With regard to the Mental Health Act, we will examine the role of the nearest relative of patients detained under the Act as well as those subject to community powers. The role of the Tribunal in reviewing detention and community powers will be explored. As it is likely, if you are working with people with a mental disorder, that you will find yourself writing a report for the Tribunal as well as presenting evidence before it, we will examine what the Tribunal will require of you. The hospital managers serve a similar function to the Tribunal and we will explore their role in the reviewing of decisions. The Care Quality Commission and the Healthcare Inspectorate in Wales have specific duties with regard to the operation of the Mental Health Act and we will briefly examine these.

The safeguards built into the Mental Capacity Act will be examined by exploring the role of a person who has been given a Lasting Power of Attorney as well as the role of the relevant person's representative. The role of the Court of Protection will be examined, both in relation to those subject to the Deprivation of Liberty Safeguards and in its wider role with regard to adults who lack capacity to make certain decisions.

Mental Health Act safeguards

The nearest relative

The nearest relative has some significant powers under the MHA, especially in relation to the longer-term provisions. However, these powers can be blocked and an application made to the County Court to displace them as the nearest relative in some circumstances. It is important to note that the person who is nearest relative is set out in statute, and it is not necessarily the person that the patient chooses as their next of kin. There are circumstances in which the nearest relative has no relationship with the patient at all and may even have behaved in a way that was detrimental to the good of the patient. The Mental Health Act 2007 has introduced the power of the patient to make an application to court for their current nearest relative to be displaced and have another appointed. However, the patient still cannot choose who they would like to be their nearest relative.

Before we consider how the Act defines the nearest relative, it is important to examine who is, and who is not, a relative within the Act. All relatives have a role to play as the approved mental health professional (AMHP) has to have regard to their views (MHA 1983, s13(1A)(b)). A person cannot be a nearest relative unless they are on the list of relatives. Relatives are defined in section 26 of the Act as:

- husband or wife (including same sex marriage) or civil partner (this includes people who have lived together as husband or wife or civil partner for at least six months)

- son or daughter

- father or mother

- brother or sister

- grandparent

- grandchild

- uncle or aunt

- nephew or niece

- any other person with whom the patient has been ordinarily resident with for at least five years

The order of the list above is important as people higher up the list take precedence over people lower down the list. But the complexity does not stop there. In deciding who is a relative, half-blood relatives are included but in-law ones are not. So your mother's sister (your aunt) would be a relative but her husband (your uncle) would not. Also, if the patient is ordinarily resident in the United Kingdom, the Channel Islands or the Isle of Man, any relatives that are not also so resident are not relatives for the purposes of the Act and do not make it onto the above list. However, if the patient is not ordinarily resident in the UK, the Channel Islands or the Isle of Man, then their relatives do not have to be so resident and should be included on the list. The Act states that illegitimate children are to be regarded as legitimate children of their mother. If the patient is under 18, the father can only be a relative if he is, or was, married to the mother of the child, or he acquires parental responsibility (PR) for the child by a range of other means. However, when the patient reaches 18, PR no longer exists (as the child is now an adult) and if the father has never married the mother, the father may no longer be a relative. This can cause problems (Barber et al., 2012: p107) as overnight the father may go from being the nearest relative (on the basis that he has PR and is the older parent) to not being a relative at all because he never married the mother of his child.

As you can see, identifying who is a relative, never mind who is the nearest relative, is not always a straightforward matter. Identifying the relatives and nearest relative is a role for the AMHP, but if you are making a referral for an assessment under the Act you need to make sure you give accurate information to the AMHP with regard to the patient's relatives so that the correct nearest relative can be quickly identified.

In deciding who is the nearest relative, the AMHP disregards any relative under the age of 18 unless they are the patient's husband, wife, civil partner or living as such, or they are the patient's parent. A husband, wife or civil partner is disregarded if they are permanently separated or divorced. The AMHP has to then highlight anyone on the list who ordinarily resides with the patient *or* provides significant care for the patient as these people take precedence. If there is more than one person living with or caring for the patient, the hierarchy above still applies to that separate group of relatives. The nearest relative is the one who appears highest on the list. If there is more than one person at the top of the list (e.g. both parents who are married to each other) then the older takes precedence over the younger and the full-blood relative takes precedence over the half-blood relative.

The nearest relative does have the right to make an application under sections 2, 3, 4 and 7 but the MHA Code of Practice discourages this practice (para 14.30) saying that the AMHP is usually the more appropriate applicant because of their professional training, knowledge of the law and local resources.

The nearest relative must be informed by the AMHP that an application is to be made, or has been made, under section 2. The AMHP has to consult the nearest relative before making an application under section 3 as the nearest relative has the right to object to such an application. If the nearest relative objects the application cannot go ahead. The AMHP can in some circumstances not consult the nearest relative but this is in very limited circumstances and only if it is not reasonably practicable or would cause unreasonable delay (MHA, s11(4)). Such situations would include when it is not possible to identify the nearest relative due to a lack of information, the nearest relative is physically or mentally unwell, or when it would be possible to consult but it would cause significant distress for the patient (MHA Code, paras 14.61–14.63).

The nearest relative also has the power to discharge the patient from detention under section 23 of the Act and the AMHP has to make sure that the nearest relative is informed of this right (MHA, s11(3)). The nearest relative has to write to the hospital giving them 72 hours' notice in writing and at the end of that period the patient must be discharged unless the responsible clinician (RC) considers that it would be 'dangerous' to discharge the patient and they block the discharge order under section 25(1). Once the nearest relative order is blocked they cannot make another discharge order for six months. However, if the patient is detained under section 3 the nearest relative can appeal to the Mental Health Tribunal against the blocking order by the RC.

The nearest relative has the right to request that the local social services authority (LSSA) consider undertaking an assessment under the Mental Health Act (MHA, s13(4)). This requires the LSSA to arrange for an AMHP to 'consider the patient's case'. This does not need to be a full assessment under the Act as long as the patient's case has been considered and other means of providing the care or treatment they need have been put in place. However, if the AMHP decides not to make an application under the MHA they need to write to the nearest relative giving their reasons.

If the nearest relative does not want to exercise these responsibilities for whatever reason, they can delegate their responsibilities under Mental Health Act regulations. The person they delegate to does not have to be a relative (as long as they are over 18; live in the UK, Channel Islands or the Isle of Man (if the patient is so resident); and not permanently separated (if husband, wife or civil partner)).

If the AMHP considers that the nearest relative's objection to an application under section 3 is unreasonable, they can apply to the County Court for the nearest relative to be displaced and another appointed. If the patient objects to their nearest relative acting as such, and the nearest relative is refusing to delegate their responsibilities, they can apply to the County Court to have their nearest relative displaced. An application to displace the nearest relative can only be based on the following grounds (MHA, s29(3)):

- there is no nearest relative within the meaning of the Act
- that the nearest relative is incapable of acting as such by reason of mental disorder or other illness
- that the nearest relative unreasonably objects to the making of an application for admission for treatment or a guardianship application
- that the nearest relative has exercised with due regard to the welfare of the patient or the interests of the public their power to discharge the patient from hospital or guardianship
- that the nearest relative of the patient is otherwise not a suitable person to act as such

The power to make an application to the County Court to displace the nearest relative is not restricted to the patient; any relative of the patient, any other person who resides with the patient or an AMHP can also make such applications. The MHA Code (para 5.12) encourages AMHPs to make an application to displace or appoint a nearest relative where there is no nearest relative or they have good reasons to think that a patient considers their nearest relative unsuitable and would like them to be replaced.

The nearest relative also has the right to be given certain information about the patient's detention under section 132 of the Act unless the patient objects. Also under section 133, the nearest relative must be given seven days' notice of the hospital's decision to discharge the patient.

Mental Health Tribunal and Mental Health Review Tribunal

The Tribunals for England and Wales are now very different. In England the tribunal service has been significantly reformed and is now part of the HM Courts and Tribunal Service. Wales has its own mental health tribunal, which is called the Mental Health Review Tribunal for Wales (MHRT). In England there is the First Tier Tribunal (Mental Health) often known as the Mental Health Tribunal (MHT). The MHRT and MHT hear applications from patients with regard to decisions to use compulsory powers. There is an Upper Tribunal that covers both England and Wales that hears appeals from the MHRT and MHT. The operation of the Tribunals is covered by Tribunal Rules and there are separate Tribunal Rules for the English and Welsh Tribunals (The Tribunal Procedure: First-Tier Tribunal. Health, Education and Social Care Chamber Rules, 2008).

The role of the Tribunal is to decide whether or not the patient should remain subject to compulsory powers. That is, at the time of the Tribunal hearing, the grounds for the compulsory powers are still met or the patient must be discharged from those powers. It also has the power to make recommendations in certain circumstances. It is not the role of the Tribunal to decide if the initial detention was lawful or appropriate. The role of the Tribunal is to uphold the Article 5(4) European Convention right of the patient to a speedy and effective review of their detention.

There are several routes by which a patient could have a hearing. The patient themselves can make an application to the Tribunal at certain stages in their detention.

Also, in certain circumstances, the nearest relative can make an application to the Tribunal. The managers of the hospital have a duty to refer cases to the Tribunal in certain circumstances. There is also discretion on behalf of the Secretary of State and the Welsh Ministers to refer cases to the Tribunal as they see fit.

When patients can apply to the Tribunal is set out in section 66 of the Act, but it is not an easy section to understand. A patient detained under section 2 can apply to the Tribunal within the first 14 days of their detention. A patient on section 3 can apply once in each period of detention, that is within the first six months, then in the second six months and then once yearly. With regard to patients subject to Part III (the mentally disordered offender provisions), the situation is a little more complicated. Patients on hospital orders can apply after the first six months but not before and then yearly.

The nearest relative of the patient can apply to the Tribunal in certain circumstances, mainly when the RC has blocked their application to discharge the patient as discussed above. They have 28 days from being told that their application has been blocked to apply to the Tribunal. Also, in the case of an unrestricted hospital order patient, the nearest relative does not have the power to discharge the patient but they do have the ability to apply to the Tribunal at the same frequency as the patient.

The hospital managers have an obligation to refer a case to the Tribunal under section 68 of the Act. They have to refer to the Tribunal if six months have lapsed since the patient was detained and the patient themself has not made an application or someone else has not referred/applied to the Tribunal on the patient's behalf. The managers have to refer a detained (unrestricted) patient or a CTO patient if three years have lapsed since their last Tribunal hearing. Also, a patient whose CTO has been revoked following recall to hospital must be referred to the Tribunal.

The Secretary of State and Welsh Ministers have a general discretion to refer a case to the Tribunal when they think fit. They do not have an obligation to do so, but they can be asked to refer a case to the Tribunal. This can be a useful way of a patient getting a Tribunal hearing if they are not otherwise entitled to a hearing.

The Tribunal hearing usually takes place in the hospital where the patient is detained, or in the case of community patients, this can be in the community team's base. There are three members of the Tribunal: the Tribunal Judge who is legally qualified and who chairs the hearing, a medical member who is usually a consultant psychiatrist (and usually undertakes a medical examination of the patient before the hearing) and a specialist member, who usually has experience in the provision of community mental health services. The judge sits in the middle with the medical member on their right and the specialist member on their left. The patient usually sits opposite the judge with their legal representative (if they have one) on their left, with the responsible clinician on the left of them opposite the medical member. On the right of the patient will sit the nurse and to the right of the nurse will be the author of the social circumstances report – usually a social worker but sometimes a community psychiatric nurse or occupational therapist. Sometimes other people may be present at the Tribunal such as relatives of the patient.

The Tribunal Rules set out how the hearing should run and what evidence can be heard. The responsible clinician and the patient's nurse have to produce reports for the Tribunal. There also needs to be a social circumstances report prepared. The latter is the responsibility of the local social services authority but is usually allocated to a social worker or the patient's care coordinator if they have one. If there is no community worker allocated to the patient then the LSSA will have to ensure they make the arrangements for a professional to complete the report. The reports are read by the Tribunal members before the hearing. The hearing usually follows a set order, with the judge starting the proceedings by explaining the proceedings to the patient, asking them, or their representative, what they are asking the Tribunal to do. The Tribunal members will try and make the proceedings as informal as possible but it still has the status of a court so certain formalities have to be followed. The judge will usually explain what the medical member has told them following their examination of the patient, if there has been one. The medical member will usually then ask questions of the responsible clinician based on their report, and then the patient or their representative will have an opportunity to ask questions of the RC. The Tribunal will then move to the nurse and their report and then to the social worker and their report in a similar pattern. The social worker is more likely to be asked questions by the specialist member. Once all the professionals have given their evidence, the patient will be asked to provide their evidence either in the form of a statement or via questions asked of them by their legal representative. The patient can also provide their own independent psychiatric or social circumstances reports. The Tribunal has a wide discretion as to how they run their hearings but they usually follow a similar format.

As a social worker working with people with a mental disorder, it is very likely that you will find yourself in front of a Tribunal presenting a social circumstances report. The information that needs to be included in a social circumstances report is set out in a Practice Direction by the Senior President of Tribunals (Tribunals Judiciary, 2013). These are regularly updated so you need to look for the latest Practice Direction. However, the main purpose for your report is to outline what support would be available for the patient should the Tribunal exercise their power to discharge them. Therefore, before any Tribunal hearing there should be a discharge-planning meeting to consider the patient's aftercare under section 117 (if eligible) and the care plan produced included in your report. Your report has to be completed and sent to the Tribunal Service within three weeks of the date that the patient applied or was referred to the Tribunal. This is a statutory requirement and if you do not complete your report within this timescale, the Tribunal has the power to impose sanctions on you or your employer.

ACTIVITY **10.1**

Format of a social circumstances report

Locate your employer's template for social circumstances reports to the Mental Health Tribunal. Compare this template with the latest Practice Direction. Does the template allow for all the information required by the Tribunal to be included? How would you ensure that you gathered and provided all the information that the Tribunal requires when you have to write a social circumstances report?

There are certain powers available to the Tribunal following a hearing. They must discharge patients if the relevant legal criteria for detention, guardianship or CTO are not met. They also have discretion to discharge patients (as long as they are not restricted patients, i.e. not subject to section 41, 45A or 49 of the Mental Health Act, see Chapter 8) even if the legal criteria for detention or use of compulsory powers are met. They can defer the discharge of a patient detained in hospital to a future date to allow arrangements to be made for their aftercare, and the patient will have to be discharged on or before that date. The Tribunal can make certain recommendations (in cases where the patient is not restricted). These are known as statutory recommendations. The Tribunal can recommend that the patient be considered for: a community treatment order; section 17 leave; transfer to another hospital; or transfer into guardianship. They do not have the power to require these things to happen but they can reconvene to reconsider the case.

The powers of the Tribunal are slightly different with reference to restricted patients. They do not have the same discretion to discharge patients even if the grounds for detention are met. They can discharge restricted patients either conditionally (subject to the power of recall by the Ministry of Justice, see Chapter 8) or absolutely (no longer subject to any compulsory powers) and they can defer the discharge to allow for aftercare arrangements to be put in place. They do not have the same power to make recommendations.

CASE STUDY

Michelle

Michelle is currently in hospital under section 3 of the Act. She has now been in hospital for just over a year. She has made an application to the Tribunal for them to discharge her from hospital. She is being supported by a legal representative. She has appealed to the Tribunal twice during this admission but they have not, to date, discharged her. Her responsible clinician does not feel that she is ready to be discharged from hospital as Michelle does not agree with him that she has a mental disorder. Her social worker has been working with Michelle for many years and feels that the risk that Michelle presents to herself has reduced sufficiently to warrant discharge. Whilst Michelle does not accept her mental disorder diagnosis, she does agree that she needs support on a day to day basis and her social worker has arranged for Michelle to move into her own accommodation with support from an organisation that Michelle chose after interviewing them. The social worker has written the social circumstances report supporting Michelle's application to be discharged from hospital.

You are Michelle's social worker. You have to speak in support of your report and answer questions at the Tribunal. How would you prepare? What arguments would you put forward to support discharge in the face of the responsible clinician's opposition?

Hospital managers

Managers of the hospital have the power to discharge unrestricted detained patients and community treatment order patients. As a result a patient can also appeal to the hospital managers against their detention or CTO. The managers can review a patient's detention at any time but must do so when the period of detention is renewed (when a section 3 or section 37 is extended for another six months or yearly) or a CTO is extended. They should also consider reviewing the detention if the RC has blocked an application by the nearest relative to discharge the patient. The criteria that the hospital managers should apply are whether the grounds for detention, or CTO, continue to be met or not. Also, if reviewing a blocking order, they need to consider whether the patient would act in a manner which would be 'dangerous' to themselves or others if they were to be discharged.

The hospital has to delegate its discharge functions to 'hospital managers' as the function of discharging patients cannot be delegated to employees or officers of the hospital. Like the Tribunal the hospital managers panel is made up of three people authorised by the hospital. There are no formal rules like the Tribunal but the hearings have to be fair. The MHA Code (para 38.34) gives guidance as to how hearings should be carried out. The managers should be provided with similar reports as for the Tribunal, and the reports should follow a similar format with the responsible clinician, nurse and social worker (or other community professional) present. A patient can be represented at a manager's hearing in the same way as for a Tribunal.

Care Quality Commission

The Care Quality Commission (CQC) as well as regulating the provision of health and social care in England has been given specific responsibilities with regard to the operation of the Mental Health Act 1983. These are set out in sections 120 to 120D of the Act. The CQC and the Healthcare Inspectorate in Wales must:

- Keep under review, and where appropriate, investigate the exercise of powers and the discharge of duties under the Mental Health Act. This relates to both patients detained in hospital and those subject to community powers.

- Make arrangements for persons authorised by it to visit and interview detained patients in private in the hospitals in which they are detained and other places as appropriate.

- Make arrangements for persons authorised by it to investigate any complaints about the discharge of any duties under the Mental Health Act.

- Publish an annual report on its activities in the exercise of its functions under the Act.

The CQC employs people with special experience in the operation of the Mental Health Act to carry out its review functions. These are now called Mental Health Act reviewers and visit hospitals on at least a yearly basis to visit detained patients and interview them in private. Mental Health Act reviewers also speak to staff of the hospital and review patient records. They produce a report to the hospital on their visit with areas on which the hospital needs to take action. These reports are used to compile the CQC's annual report on the operation of the Act (CQC, 2014). These reports are recommended reading for anyone working within the provisions of the Mental Health Act.

Mental Capacity Act safeguards

Lasting Power of Attorney and deputies

The Mental Capacity Act provides for a person to donate to another person or persons the power to make decisions on their behalf for a time when they lose the capacity to make those decisions for themselves. This is called a Lasting Power of Attorney (LPA) and replaced the previous Enduring Power of Attorney provisions. A person can only make an LPA if they have the capacity to make the decision to donate the power of attorney. If the person has lost capacity to decide to donate an LPA, an LPA cannot be made. Instead the Court of Protection can be asked to appoint a deputy or deputies to carry out a similar role.

There are two types of LPA both defined in section 9(1) of the Mental Capacity Act 2005: a personal welfare LPA and a property and affairs LPA. However, the Act does not set out the scope of these LPAs. The MCA Code (para 7.21) states that a personal welfare LPA can include healthcare and medical treatment decisions and such decisions might include:

- where the donor should live and who they should live with
- the donor's day-to-day care, including diet and dress
- who the donor may have contact with
- consenting to or refusing medical examination and treatment on the donor's behalf
- assessments for and provision of community care services
- whether the donor should take part in social activities, leisure activities, education or training
- the donor's personal correspondence and papers
- rights of access to personal information about the donor, or
- complaints about the donor's care or treatment

There are certain limitations on the decisions the donee of a personal welfare LPA can make on behalf of the donor. A donee of such an LPA cannot make healthcare decisions if the donor has stated clearly in the LPA that they do not want the attorney (donee) to make these decisions (MCA Code, para 7.26). If the donor has the capacity to make a particular healthcare decision then the attorney does not have the power to make that particular decision (MCA, s11(7)(a)). If there is a valid and applicable advance decision to refuse a specific treatment (discussed in Chapter 6) then the donee cannot consent to the treatment that is the subject of the advance decision. However, if the LPA was made after the advance decision (and the LPA authorises healthcare decisions) the advance decision is invalidated (MCA, s25(2)(b)) and the donee can choose not to follow the advance decision (MCA Code, para 7.27). If the decision relates to life-sustaining treatment then the LPA needs to specifically authorise the donee to make such decisions (MCA, s11(7)(c), s11(8)). The donee cannot consent or refuse treatment for a mental disorder where the patient is detained under the

Mental Health Act (MCA, s28). Donees cannot make decisions that would result in the donor being deprived of their liberty (MCA Code, para 7.44).

With regard to property and affairs, the decisions that the donee can make include (MCA Code, para 7.36):

- buying or selling property
- opening, closing or operating any bank, building society or other account
- giving access to the donor's financial information
- claiming, receiving and using (on the donor's behalf) all benefits, pensions, allowances and rebates
- receiving any income, inheritance or other entitlement on behalf of the donor
- dealing with the donor's tax affairs
- paying the donor's mortgage, rent and household expenses
- insuring, maintaining and repairing the donor's property
- investing the donor's savings
- making limited gifts on the donor's behalf
- paying for private medical care and residential care or nursing home fees
- applying for any entitlement to funding for NHS care, social care or adaptations
- using the donor's money to buy a vehicle or any equipment or other help they need
- repaying interest and capital on any loan taken out by the donor

Both types of LPA need to be registered with the Office of the Public Guardian who maintain a register of LPAs before they can come into force. However, once a property and affairs LPA is registered (unless the donor states otherwise), the donee can make decisions about the donor's property and affairs even if the donor retains the capacity to make these decisions (MCA Code, para 7.32).

Donees of LPAs are in a position to make significant decisions of behalf of vulnerable adults without much oversight and as such there are increased opportunities for abuse (Brown et al., 2009: p42). Donees are subject to the principles in section 1 of the Act including only making decisions in the donor's best interests (MCA Code, para 7.53) and the Court of Protection does have the power to remove an attorney if they do not act in the donor's best interests (MCA Code, para 7.45). Attorneys must keep records of their dealings with the donor's affairs and the Court of Protection can order them to produce these records (MCA Code, para 7.49). As a social worker working with a vulnerable adult, you may be aware that the person has made an LPA. If you suspect that an attorney is not acting in the donor's best interest, you must consider invoking your employer's adult safeguarding procedures.

The Court of Protection has the power to appoint a deputy to make decisions on behalf of a person who lacks capacity to make decisions about their property or welfare. However, it will only do this when it is not practicable for the court to make the decision itself. This could include situations: when there is a range of difficult decisions that need to be made over a period of time; where family members cannot agree over what is in the person's best interests; or where there are regular irreconcilable differences between health and social care professionals and the relatives of the person (Brown et al., 2009: p53).

The powers of a specific deputy are given to them by the court and they cannot act outside those powers. The court can appoint a deputy to make decisions about property and affairs or personal welfare (MCA Code, para 8.35). The deputy cannot make decisions in certain situations (MCA, s20):

- if they do something that is intended to restrain the person who lacks capacity
- if they think the person has capacity to make the particular decision
- if their decision goes against the decision made by a donee of an LPA
- about the provision or continuation of life-sustaining treatment (these need to be made by the court)

Relevant person's representative

The relevant person's representative (RPR) is only relevant to the Deprivation of Liberty Safeguards (DOLS) provisions within the MCA and is akin to the nearest relative provisions within the MHA except their powers are much more limited and they are appointed after the standard authorisation is made (see Chapter 9 for a fuller discussion on DOLS).

The supervisory body must appoint an RPR for every person to whom they give a standard authorisation. This has to be done at the time the authorisation is given or as soon as possible afterwards (DOLS Code, para 7.1). It is the role of the best interests assessor (BIA) to recommend to the supervisory body who should be the RPR. The requirements for an RPR are that they are: 18 years old or over, able to keep in contact with the relevant person (the person who is subject to the standard authorisation) and willing to be appointed (DOLS Code, para 7.6). If the relevant person has the capacity to select their own representative and selects a person who meets the above requirements, the BIA must recommend that person to be RPR. If the person does not have the capacity to make this decision, then a donee or deputy with the appropriate authority may select who should be recommended as the RPR. In making their decision who to recommend as the RPR the BIA should consider (DOLS Code, para 7.16):

- Does the relevant person have a preference?
- If they do not have the capacity to express a preference now, is there any written statement made by the relevant person when they had capacity that indicates who they may now want to be their representative?
- Will the proposed representative be able to keep in contact with the relevant person?
- Does the relevant person appear to trust and feel comfortable with the proposed representative?

- Would the proposed representative be able to represent the relevant person effectively?

- Is the proposed representative likely to represent the relevant person's best interests?

The RPR has certain rights and the supervisory body should make sure that they are aware of these rights. The supervisory body should inform the relevant person and their representative of (DOLS Code, para 7.4):

- the effect of the authorisation

- their right to request a review of the standard authorisation

- the formal and informal complaints procedures that are available to them

- their right to make an application to the Court of Protection to seek variation or termination of the authorisation, and

- their right, where the relevant person does not have a paid 'professional' representative, to request the support of an independent mental capacity advocate (IMCA)

The supervisory body has to ensure that both the relevant person and their representative understand these rights. As a social worker involved in such a case, it is important that you keep in touch with the RPR and support them and the relevant person to understand their rights, but more importantly, support them in exercising these rights.

If there is no one who can act as the person's RPR then the supervisory body has to appoint a paid representative. In most cases this will be part of the local authority's contract with the IMCA service and a professional representative will be IMCA trained.

Court of Protection

The new Court of Protection was established following the implementation of section 45(1) of the MCA. Prior to this there was also a Court of Protection that was much less powerful and more limited in its powers than the current court. As the new Court of Protection sits at the same level in the court system as the High Court (see Chapter 1), it has the same powers, rights and powers of the High Court (MCA Code, para 8.2). As a result its decisions are binding on lower courts and public authorities in carrying out their duties under the MCA.

The Court of Protection deals with all issues concerning people who lack capacity to make specific decisions for themselves. It can make decisions in relation to: a person's property and affairs; issues of personal welfare; making of medical decisions including resolving ethical dilemmas and issues around life-sustaining treatment; applications to challenge powers of LPAs; authorising deprivation of liberty; determining living arrangements; resolving issues of who should have contact with an incapacitated person; and deciding who should consent or refuse medical treatment on behalf of the person (Brown et al., 2009: 71).

The court has the power to make declarations, decisions and orders in relation to financial and welfare matters affecting people who lack, or are alleged to lack, capacity in relation to specific decisions (MCA Code, para 8.13). Section 15 of the MCA provides the court with powers to make a ruling on specific issues. These include whether or not the person has the capacity to make certain decisions. Also the court can decide whether or not a specific act in relation to a person's care or treatment is lawful. This could include a decision to withdraw that treatment which may lead to the person's death. These 'serious healthcare and treatment decisions' include (MCA Code, para 8.18):

- decisions about the proposed withholding or withdrawal of artificial nutrition and hydration (ANH) from patients in a permanent vegetative state (PVS)
- cases involving organ or bone marrow donation by a person who lacks capacity to consent
- cases involving the proposed non-therapeutic sterilisation of a person who lacks capacity to consent to this (e.g. for contraceptive purposes) and
- all other cases where there is a doubt or dispute about whether a particular treatment will be in a person's best interests

The court can also appoint deputies to make decisions for people who lack the capacity to make them and it can remove deputies or attorneys who act inappropriately (MCA Code, para 8.13). It can also make decisions where there are concerns about the validity and applicability of an advance directive (MCA Code, para 8.28).

The Court of Protection also has a role with regard to the operation of Deprivation of Liberty Safeguards. In order to comply with Article 5(4) of the European Convention on Human Rights, the state has to ensure that a person has the right of speedy access to a court to determine if their deprivation of liberty is lawful or not. For the purposes of DOLS the Court of Protection is such a court. The court plays a similar role to the Mental Health Tribunal in the cases of patients subject to Mental Health Act powers.

A relevant person (or someone acting on their behalf) can apply to the court before a decision is made with regard to a standard authorisation. This may be to declare that the person has the capacity to make a decision to reside in the care home or hospital for the purposes of receiving care or treatment. It could also be to decide whether or not the proposed actions are lawful, i.e. are in the person's best interests.

However, it is more common for an application to the court to be made after the standard or urgent authorisation is in place. Both the relevant person and the RPR have the automatic right to apply to the court to challenge decisions made by the supervisory body or managing authority. These include (DOLS Code, para 10.2):

- whether or not the six qualifying requirements are met (age, no refusals, capacity, mental health, eligibility, best interests)
- the period for which the standard authorisation is to be in force
- the purpose for which the standard authorisation is given
- the conditions attached to the standard authorisation

The Court of Protection can vary or terminate the standard or urgent authorisation, or it can direct the supervisory body or the managing authority to vary or terminate the authorisation (DOLS Code, para 10.10).

As DOLS only relate to care homes or hospitals, if a person who lacks capacity to make decisions about their care is deprived of their liberty in another setting (supported living or in their own home) an application will be need to be made to the court for this to be authorised (DOLS Code, para 10.11).

The Court of Protection provides significant safeguards for people who lack the capacity to make certain decisions (or it is thought that they might lack capacity). As a social worker working with vulnerable adults, it is important that the people you are working with understand their rights to apply to the court or have other people to make applications on their behalf. Also, you need to recognise when a decision or action in regard to a person who lacks capacity falls outside of your powers (and that of your employer) under the MCA, and make arrangements for the case to be considered by the Court of Protection.

CHAPTER SUMMARY

- For patients detained or being assessed under the Mental Health Act, the nearest relative provides significant safeguards including the power to object to an application for admission for treatment (section 3) and the power to require that the patient be discharged (Part II patients only).
- The Mental Health Tribunal and Mental Health Review Tribunal for Wales have significant powers with regard to patients subject to the MHA, including the power to order a patient's discharge from compulsory powers.
- Hospital managers have the power to discharge certain patients from compulsory powers.
- The Care Quality Commission has specific responsibilities with regard to patients subject to the MHA including visiting patients in private.
- Lasting Power of Attorney and deputies have the power to make decisions on behalf of people who lack the capacity to make these decisions for themselves.
- The relevant person's representative has important safeguards with regard to a person subject to DOLS in a similar way that a nearest relative has over a patient detained under the MHA.
- The Court of Protection has wide-ranging powers with regard to deciding matters to do with people who lack the capacity to make specific decisions for themselves.

FURTHER READING

Department of Constitutional Affairs (2007) *Mental Capacity Act 2005 Code of Practice*. London: TSO.
Chapter 7 gives guidance on Lasting Powers of Attorney; Chapter 8 on the Court of Protection; and Chapter 10 on the role of the independent mental capacity advocate.

Department of Health (2015) *Mental Health Act 1983: Code of Practice*. London: TSO.
Chapter 5 gives guidance on the role of the nearest relative and Chapter 12 on the Tribunal.

Appendix: Professional Capabilities Framework

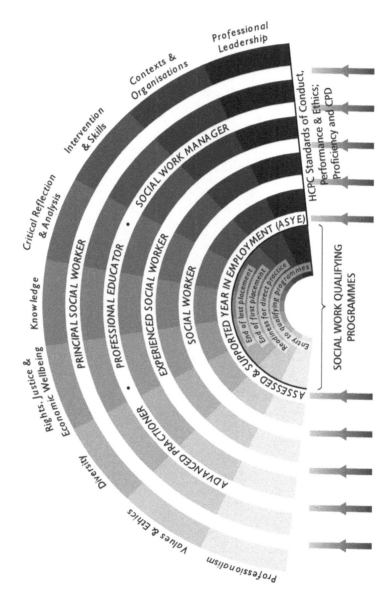

Professional Capabilities Framework diagram reproduced with permission of The College of Social Work

Bibliography

Statutes

Care Act 2014

Care Standards Act 2000

Coroners and Justice Act 2009

County Asylums Act 1808

Criminal Justice Act 2003

Criminal Procedure (Insanity) Act 1964

Criminal Procedure (Insanity and Unfitness to Plead) Act 1991

Domestic Violence Crime and Victims Act 2004

European Convention on Human Rights 1950

Health and Social Care Act 2012

Homicide Act 1957

Human Rights Act 1998

Lunacy Act 1890

Lunatics Act 1845

Madhouses Act 1774

Mental Capacity Act 2005

Mental Deficiency Act 1913

Mental Health (Approved Mental Health Professionals) (Approval) (England) Regulations 2008

Mental Health (Hospital, Guardianship and Treatment) Regulations 1983

Mental Health (Hospital, Guardianship, Community Treatment and Consent to Treatment) (Wales) Regulations 2008

Mental Health Act 1959

Mental Health Act 1983

Mental Health Act 2007

Mental Health Act Regulations 1983

Mental Health Review Tribunal for Wales Rules 2008

Mental Treatment Act 1930

National Assistance Act 1948

Police and Criminal Evidence Act 1984

Poor Law Amendment Act 1834

Poor Relief Act 1601

The Tribunal Procedure (First-Tier Tribunal) (Health, Education and Social Care Chamber) Rules 2008

Trial of Criminal Lunatics Act 1883

Tribunals Judiciary (2013) Practice Direction: First-Tier Tribunal Health Education and Social Care Chamber, statements and reports in mental health cases

Vagrancy Act 1744

Case law

A Local Authority v E and Ors [2012] EWHC 1639 (COP)

Airedale Hospital Trustees v Bland [1992] UKHL 5

Bolam v Friern Hospital Management Committee [1957] 2 All ER 118

HL v UK [2004] 40 EHHR 761

Kay v UK 17821/91 [1994] ECHR 51

LB Hillingdon v Steven Neary and others [2011] EWHC 1377 (COP)

M'Naughten (1843) 10 C & F 200

P v Cheshire West and Chester Council and another, P and Q v Surrey County Council [2014] UKSC 19

Storck v Germany (61603/00) [2005] 1 MHLR 211

Re C (adult: refusal of medical treatment) [1994] 1 All ER 819

Re T [1992] 4 All ER 649

R (Munjaz) v Mersey Care NHS Trust [2005] UKHL 58

R v Barnet LBC ex parte Shah [1983] 1 All ER 226

Sidaway v Board of Bethlem Royal Hospital [1985] 1 All ER 643

The NHS Trust v L and Ors [2012] EWHC 2741 (COP)

Winterwerp v Netherlands [1979] 2 EHHR 387

Official materials

American Psychiatric Association (2013) *Diagnostic and Statistical Manual*, 5th edition. American Psychiatric Publishing

Bradley, K (2009) *The Bradley Report: Lord Bradley's Review of People with Mental Health Problems or Learning Disabilities in the Criminal Justice System*. London: Department of Health

Care Council for Wales (undated) *Code of Practice for Social Care Workers*. Cardiff: Care Council for Wales

Care Quality Commission (2014) *Monitoring the Mental Health Act in 2012/13*. London: Care Quality Commission

Department of Constitutional Affairs (2007) *Mental Capacity Act 2005 Code of Practice*. London: TSO

Department of Health (1999) *National Service Framework for Mental Health.* London: TSO

Department of Health (2008) *Refocusing the Care Programme Approach: Policy and Positive Practice Guidance.* London: TSO

Department of Health (2015a) *Mental Health Act 1983: Code of Practice.* London: TSO

Department of Health (2015b) *Reference Guide to the Mental Health Act 1983.* London: TSO

Health and Care Professions Council (2012) *Standards of Proficiency for Social Workers in England.* London: Health and Care Professions Council

Health and Social Care Information Centre (2014) *Inpatients Formally Detained in Hospitals under the Mental Health Act 1983, and Patients Subject to Supervised Community Treatment: Annual Report, England 2013/14.* Leeds: HSCIC

Home Office (2014) *Revised Code of Practice for the Detention, Treatment and Questioning of Persons by Police Officers. Police And Criminal Evidence Act 1984 (PACE) – Code C.* London: TSO

House of Lords Select Committee on the Mental Capacity Act 2005 (2014) *Mental Capacity Act 2005: Post-legislative Scrutiny: HL Paper 139.* London: TSO

Law Commission (2014) *Mental Capacity and Detention* http://lawcommission.justice.gov.uk/areas/capacity-and-detention.htm (last accessed 27 October 2014)

Ministry of Justice (2008) *Mental Capacity Act 2005 Deprivation of Liberty Safeguards Code of Practice to Supplement the Main Mental Capacity Act 2005 Code of Practice.* London: TSO

Ministry of Justice (2009) *Guidance for Social Supervisors* https://www.justice.gov.uk/downloads/offenders/mentally-disordered-offenders/guidance-for-social-supervisors-0909.pdf (last accessed 19 September 2014)

Ministry of Justice (2014) *Multi-agency Public Protection Arrangements* https://www.gov.uk/government/publications/multi-agency-public-protection-arrangements-mappa--2 (last accessed 19 September 2014)

NHS London (2009) *Independent Inquiry into the Care and Treatment of Peter Bryan and Richard Loudwell*

Office of the Deputy Prime Minister (2004) *Mental Health and Social Exclusion: Social Exclusion Unit Report.* London: HMSO

Welsh Assembly Government (2008) *Mental Health Act 1983 Code of Practice for Wales.* Cardiff: Welsh Assembly Government

World Health Organisation (1992) *International Classification of Diseases, 10th edition.* Geneva: World Health Organisation

Books

Barber, P, Brown, R and Martin, D (2012) *Mental Health Law in England and Wales,* 2nd edition. London: Sage/Learning Matters

Bartlett, P and Sandland, R (2014) *Mental Health Law Policy and Practice,* 4th edition. Oxford: Oxford University Press

Bentall, R (2003) *Madness Explained: Psychosis and Human Nature.* London: Penguin

Beresford, P (2005) Social Approaches to Madness and Distress, in Tew, J (ed) *Social Perspectives in Mental Health.* London: Jessica Kingsley

Bingham, T (2010) *The Rule of Law.* London: Penguin Books

Bogg, D (2010) *Values and Ethics in Mental Health Practice.* Exeter: Learning Matters

British Medical Association (1992) *Medicine Betrayed.* London: Zed Books

Brown, R (2009) *Approved Mental Health Professionals Guide to Mental Health Law*, 2nd edition. Exeter: Learning Matters

Brown, R, Barber, P and Martin, D (2009) *The Mental Capacity Act 2005: A Guide for Practice*, 2nd edition. Exeter: Learning Matters

Carr, S (2005) Lesbian and Gay Perspectives on Mental Distress, in Tew, J (ed) *Social Perspectives in Mental Health.* London: Jessica Kingsley

Davis, D and Neal, C (1996) *Pink Therapy.* Buckingham: Open University Press

Double, D (2005) Beyond Biomedical Models, in Tew, J (ed) *Social Perspectives in Mental Health.* London: Jessica Kingsley

Fennell, P (2010) Mental Health Law: History, Policy and Regulation, in Gostin, L, Bartlett, P, Fennell, P, McHale, J and Mackay, R (eds) *Principles of Mental Health Law and Policy.* Oxford: Oxford University Press

Fennell, P (2011) *Mental Health Law and Practice*, 2nd edition. Bristol: Jordans

Ferns, P (2005) Finding a Way Forward: A Black Perspective, in Tew, J (ed) *Social Perspectives in Mental Health.* London: Jessica Kingsley

Finch, E and Fafinski, S (2009) *Legal Skills*, 2nd edition. Oxford: Oxford University Press

Hale, B (2010) *Mental Health Law*, 5th edition. London: Sweet & Maxwell

Heller, T, Reynolds, J, Gomm, R, Muston, R and Pattison, S (1996) *Mental Health Matters.* Basingstoke: Macmillan

Jones, R (2012) *Mental Capacity Act Handbook,* 5th edition. London: Sweet & Maxwell

Jones, R (2013) *Mental Health Act Handbook*, 16th edition. London: Sweet & Maxwell

King, M and McKeown, E (2003) *Mental Health and Social Wellbeing of Gay Men, Lesbians and Bisexuals in England and Wales.* London: Mind

Neary, M (2011) *Get Steven Home.* Lulu.com

Read, J and Reynolds, J (eds) (1996) *Speaking Our Minds: An Anthology.* Basingstoke: Macmillan

Rogers, A and Pilgrim, D (2010) *A Sociology of Mental Health and Illness*, 4th edition. Maidenhead: Open University Press

Rutter, R and Brown, K (2012) *Critical Thinking and Professional Judgement for Social Work.* London: Sage/Learning Matters

Tew, J (2005) *Social Perspectives in Mental Health.* London: Jessica Kingsley

Webber, M (2008) *Evidence-Based Policy and Practice in Mental Health Social Work.* Exeter: Learning Matters

Williams, J (2005) Women's Mental Health: Taking Inequality into Account, in Tew, J (ed) *Social Perspectives in Mental Health.* London: Jessica Kingsley

Wise, S (2012) *Inconvenient People: Lunacy, Liberty and Mad-Doctors in Victorian England.* London: The Bodley Head

Journal articles

Burns, T, Rugkasa, J, Molodynski, A, Dawson, J, Yeeles, K, Vazquez-Montes, M, Vossey, M, Sinclair, J and Prieve, S (2013) Community treatment orders for patients with psychosis (OCTET): a randomised controlled trial. *The Lancet*, Vol 231, Issue 9878, p1627

Roberts, G, Dorkins, E, Wooldridge, J and Hewis, E (2008) Detained – what's my choice? Part 1: Discussion. *Advances in Psychiatric Treatment*, Vol 14, pp172–80

Websites

British and Irish Legal Information Institute www.bailii.org (last accessed 6 August 2014)

Community Care (2014) Deprivation of Liberty Safeguards breaching legal timescales www.communitycare.co.uk/2014/10/01/50-deprivation-liberty-safeguards-cases-breaching-legal-timescales (last accessed 27 October 2014)

Connecting People Study http://connectingpeoplestudy.net (last accessed 22 August 2014)

Court of Protection (2012) Applications to the Court of Protection in relation to tenancy agreements www.mentalhealthlaw.co.uk/images/COP_guidance_on_tenancy_agreements_February_2012.pdf (last accessed 29 October 2014)

www.legislation.gov.uk (last accessed 4 August 2014)

Mental Health Alliance (2010) Briefing Paper 2: Supervised Community Treatment www.mentalhealthalliance.org.uk/resources/SCT_briefing_paper.pdf (last accessed 5 December 2014)

Mental Health Law Online http://mentalhealthlaw.co.uk (last accessed 4 August 2014)

Mental Health Law Online http://mentalhealthlaw.co.uk/Mental_Health_Act_2007_Overview (last accessed 4 August 2014)

National Appropriate Adult Network (2014) Vulnerable Adults Policy www.appropriateadult.org.uk/index.php/policy1/vulnerable-adults (last accessed 18 September 2014)

Oxford Dictionaries www.oxforddictionaries.com/definition/english/culpability (last accessed 17 September 2014)

Oxford Dictionaries www.oxforddictionaries.com/definition/english/law (last accessed 4 August 2014)

Royal College of Psychiatrists (2014) Information about ECT (electro-convulsive therapy) www.rcpsych.ac.uk/healthadvice/treatmentswellbeing/ect.aspx (last accessed 13 October 2014)

The Equality and Human Rights Commission (2014) www.equalityhumanrights.com/your-rights/human-rights/what-are-human-rights/human-rights-act (last accessed 8 August 2014)

The Free Legal Dictionary http://legal-dictionary.thefreedictionary.com/mens+rea (last accessed 17 September 2014)

Webber, M (2014) Building the evidence base for mental health social work practice http://martinwebber.net/archives/1421 (last accessed 22 August 2014)

Index

Index

false85, 148; and restriction orders 125; role of
51; and treatment against the patients will
89–90; and the Tribunal 151
restraint 77, 96–7
restricted patients: and DOLS 140; and the
Tribunal 125, 152
restriction direction 127
restriction orders 122, 124–5, 129
restriction, use of least restrictive options 59,
63, 69, 75
reviews, section 117 105
rights: of detained patients 85–7, 98, 149;
European Convention on Human Rights
(ECHR) 18–19, 26, 37, 38–9, 108, 132,
149; human rights 25, 108; Human Rights
Act 1998 (HRA) 18–19; to liberty 132; to
liberty and security of the person 37; of
relevant person's representative (RPR) 157;
to respect private/family life 38–9; of service
users 64; of vulnerable adults 25
risk, and mentally disordered offenders 124
R (Munjaz) v Mersey Care NHS Trust [2005]
UKHL 58 47
Roberts et al. 66
Rogers, A. and Pilgrim, D. 29
Royal Assent 6, 8
rule of law 4
R v Barnet LBC ex parte Shah [1983] 1 All ER
226 103–4

safeguarding, vulnerable people 64
safeguards: MCA 154–9; MHA 146–53; nearest
relative (NR) 159; within statutes 25
secondary legislation 6, 9
second opinion approved doctor (SOAD) 51, 90,
91, 109
Secretary of State for Justice: power to recall
128, 129; power to transfer from prison
to hospital 123, 127; and restricted
patients 125
section 2, MHA 75, 78, 148, 150
section 3, MHA 75, 76, 78, 103, 148, 150
section 4, MHA 76, 87
section 5, MHA 78, 87
section 7, MHA 105
section 17, MHA 101–3, 105, 140
section 23, MHA 124, 148
section 25(1), MHA 148
section 35, MHA 101, 123
section 36, MHA 101, 123
section 37/41, MHA 124, 128
section 37, MHA 103, 107, 108, 122, 124
section 38, MHA 101, 125
section 41, MHA 101, 122, 124
section 45A, MHA 101, 103, 125
section 47, MHA 103, 127
section 48, MHA 103, 123
section 49, MHA 101, 127
section 57, MHA 90, 91

section 58, MHA 90
section 62, MHA 90, 91
section 117, MHA 101, 103–5, 111, 151
section 131, MCA 74
section 132, MHA 149
section 133, MHA 149
section 135, MHA 87
section 135(1), MHA 79, 82, 103
section 136, MHA 80, 82, 87
self-harm, in custody 117
service user movement 32
service users: Black 31; and information/consent
28; perspective of 32–3; rights of 64; voice
of 25
sexual orientation, and psychiatry 41
Sidaway v Board of Bethlem Royal Hospital
[1985] 1 All ER 643 26
social care law 4
social circumstances report 151
social control, psychiatry as 29, 30–1
social disadvantage, and mental illness 29
social inclusion agenda 30
social models, of mental disorder 29–32
social supervision, of conditionally discharged
patients 128–9
social work: decision-making in 58; evidence
base for 30; professional standards 64;
roots of 22
social workers: duties and powers of 17; duty
to uphold patient rights 85; and rights of
vulnerable adults 25; subject to judicial
review 16
'special verdict' 122
standard authorisation, DOLS 138–41, 158–9
standards of proficiency (SoP) 64
statutes 5, 7–9
statutory duties and powers 17
statutory instruments 9
sufficient information, and consent 26, 28
superior courts 15
supervision, compulsory 125
supervisory body (SB), DOLS 53, 138, 139
supported living environments, and DOLS
142, 144
surgical implantation of hormones 91
survivor movements, voice of 25

tenancy agreements, and capacity 142–3
Tew, J. 29, 30
The NHS Trust v L and Ors [2012] EWHC 2741
(COP) 7
transfer direction 127
treatment see also medical treatment:
admission for 75–6; and best interests
decision-making 94; with medication 90;
against the patients will 89–90; purpose/
effectiveness of 61; without consent 75, 76,
86, 88, 102, 110, 123
trespass, and entering patients homes 79

true174